T0194816

IT'S TIME
To Lighten Up

WHITE WILLOW

BALBOA.PRESS
A DIVISION OF HAY HOUSE

Balboa Press books may be ordered through booksellers or by contacting:

Balboa Press
A Division of Hay House
1663 Liberty Drive
Bloomington, IN 47403
www.balboapress.com
844-682-1282

Print information available on the last page.

ISBN: 979-8-7652-4253-7 (sc)
ISBN: 979-8-7652-4254-4 (hc)
ISBN: 979-8-7652-4255-1 (e)

Library of Congress Control Number: 2023909900

Balboa Press rev. date: 06/02/2023

I want to thank all the soul-centered colleagues, clients, friends, and relatives who nudged me to write my story down. I appreciate your confidence in my words. An extra special thanks for my papa, Hugo, for loving me unconditionally throughout my life. You're an exemplary human being, Papa! I love you! To my mother, Julia, who taught me to rise above the opinions of others and be my authentic self, based in heart and soul. You are my greatest teacher, Mama! I love and miss you! To my beloved sister, Monique, you inspire me to be a better human being. To my lifelong friends who listened and accepted my heart, mind, and soul at first sight: Trina, Vivi, Karen, and Giselle. Without my soul sisters, my life would never be as rich as it is. Thank you. I love you with my entire being!

To those who continue to see the world as a competitive place, this book is for you. May you gain one glimpse of wisdom from these pages: the truth that you are more powerful, capable, and loving than you can ever imagine! Rise up and discover your true nature. I see you!

With deep reverence for humanity, I bow to your potential.

In love,
White Willow (a.k.a. Virginia Biasizzo)

CONTENTS

Disclaimer ix
Preface xi

Section 1

Chapter 1 Light 1
Chapter 2 Body Pathways 11
Chapter 3 Basic Needs 25
Chapter 4 Old Meets New 34
Chapter 5 The Light of Life 45

Section 2

Chapter 6 A Purified Heart 57
Chapter 7 Can I Get a Witness? 70
Chapter 8 A Long and Winding Road 78
Chapter 9 It's All Energy 87

Section 3

Chapter 10 A New Day Dawning 99
Chapter 11 Reflecting Sets Our Compass on Course 110
Chapter 12 A New Paradigm Emerging 119

Conclusion 137

DISCLAIMER

Energy healing does not mean curing. An energy healer is a healing artist. One who creatively seeks to enhance beauty and vitality though heightened levels of intentional thought expression. Thoughts are energy. Energy is information we subconsciously communicate with.

Curing is the act of eliminating signs of illness. Curing belongs to the realm of neolithic medicine. For all purposes, this book is designated to the art of healing. Art is the expression of human creative skills coupled with imagination in producing an appreciation for their beauty and emotional power.

I have been dedicated to the healing arts for more than forty years, delighting in helping more people feel amazingly empowered. I creatively seek to enhance my understanding of the human energy field, physiological structures, and emotional patterns to help people feel better. For this reason, this book is in no way offering diagnosis, treatment, or cure for any health issues. Please consult your health-care provider for all your medical needs.

PREFACE

If I could share one thing with everyone, it would be this: *we are light.*

Literally, we emit light from every cell in our body. This light is information communicating with our collective cellular matrix, instructing every cell, atom, and subatomic particle within us in how to function normally. When we infuse our bodies with light, we nourish the light element within us that generates energy, fueling our cells with the power they need to perform and function properly. We feel and look amazing.

For most people, light emerging isn't even part of their knowledge base. There are little to no educational or social platforms that talk of our light. It's considered metaphysical and mystical or too abstract to fathom. It's been removed from ancient teachings and replaced with insights that lead us to believe we need something outside ourselves to feel better. A pill or a capsule, a drink, or a drug. Something we need to buy and consume to feel good. These are guised as remedies to take away our bad feelings and replace them with upbeat feelings.

I must share, more people are seeking alternatives to this lifestyle and medical model. The supplemental market has hit the trillion-dollar market with no end in sight. Antiaging products are leading the way. Everyone wants to lead a healthy, long life. Isn't it time we got the facts on how to do so?

The human longevity project shows there are very basic ingredients to live a long and happy life. Pure foods, water, and air along with kindhearted social exchanges are the foundation. The social aspect, sharing with others who are living a healthy lifestyle, supports the overall structure of each individual as well as the whole community.

It's well known in smaller villages and towns across the globe that when we think of ourselves as integral parts of the whole, we flourish together as one. We are only as weak as our weakest link, or as unhealthy as our sickest neighbor.

Consider the body and how it integrates with those in our family, our community, and our state. Ah! Is that too much to expand upon? OK! Let's break it down into a smaller scope.

A world-famous book says, "Let there be light," and there was light. Light is the information structure of all matter. It ignites an electron transference, a transportation of information, a coded message enacted through form. It redeems the notion of a unified field, a universal source manifesting into form.

The same is true in the body—your body, my body, everyone's body. The difference is that we've been told our body must be under the care of a physician. In case you didn't know, the word *physician* comes from the term *physicist,* a practitioner of natural science. The body is in truth a natural scientific phenomenon.

Hippocrates studied physics and natural science and is considered the father of modern medicine. He is responsible for the well-known Hippocratic oath doctors around the world swear to uphold. A legal promise to do no harm.

Yet most medications on the market come with a list of attributes known as side effects that do more harm than good. What if we chose to look at health from a new perspective? One of a healthy whole person rather than an ill individual. Focusing on the necessities to cultivate a thriving internal environment essential in prolonging wellness requires changing one's view from illness to wellness. This alternative perspective leads to new insights barely visible from the previous vantage point. New insights lead to innovative solutions for outdated ailments.

I chose this stance at an early age. Looking at the body, knowing that my body is my domain. My area to house my higher self. A safe place to dream, play, and act in any way I chose. That is if my body cooperated. Well, I have to say, I've been blessed to have a body that recovers quickly and is resilient to most adverse elements I've encountered. However, it wasn't always that way.

I was a sickly kid continuously battling a chest cold in the fall and spring seasons. There were a few years I had a cycle of pneumonias I couldn't shake. From age eight until twelve, I was sickly. Our family doctor would come to the house every Friday afternoon and shoot my butt up with penicillin. Yup, the docs made house calls back then. My folks kept the doc on salary for that stretch of time.

Funny how having an ailment can lead us to talk about it repeatedly, allowing it to define who we are. Locking us into a mental mindset of rehearsing how we are feeling and how we are going to feel repeatedly. I've heard that doing the same thing again and again while expecting a different result is a classic definition of insanity. Well, I was being primed for mental health to set in. After all, it ran in the family.

Mom had her diagnosis, which I'm pretty sure wasn't real, and my poor sister got sucked into believing that mental illness was genetic. I'm happy to say I dodged that bullet, only, it took me years to figure it out. I remember being eighteen and thinking, *Geez! When is it going to kick in? When am I going to lose my mind like the rest of the ladies in my family?*

I've been blessed to recognize genetics has absolutely nothing to do with our health, as much as we've been led to believe. It's the environment that makes us depressed or diabetic, have inflammation or heart disease, etc. The internal and external environment changes how we feel, and these feelings change how our body produces proteins and of course how our body communicates through light. Happy thoughts emit greater light capacity, and conversely negative thoughts drag us down, vary protein production, and diminish our light.

Is it starting to make sense how important understanding we are light really is? Think about it. If we taught kids that being happy is going to charge their battery cells so they have energy to feel great to run and play, *wouldn't there be happier kids?* And if kids were bummed out with low energy but there was a quick fix, wouldn't you want that quick fix for your kids? If we could go watch a funny movie, jump on a trampoline, or run outside for three minutes to recharge, wouldn't we see more kids smiling and laughing than taking meds? Wouldn't that produce healthier, happier adults?

What about the kids who are slow or unable to focus? What if I told you their brain wasn't getting the right amount of nutrition in the form of proteins or light emissions? Do you think a fair number of moms would change their kids' diets and get them out in the sun more? Believe it or not, our bodies are amazingly resilient and able to repair most ailments. That is once we start looking at how our body uses light to convert nutrients essential for living a happy, healthy life.

This book is an attempt to share what I've learned over the years researching and practicing energy healing as a natural DNA therapy practitioner and acupuncturist trained in digestion and immunogenetics. Sharing how the body uses food and light to convert proteins for normal cell functions to occur is my main goal.

Thank you for taking time to learn what has been kept separate from modern medicine for many reasons. There is countless evidence of all the insights I am sharing within these pages on several platforms, including but not limited to WebMD, Google Scholar, NIH, and our Facebook group, Energy Medicine Exchange.

SECTION 1

Body Basics

CHAPTER 1

Light

Light or visible light is considered electromagnetic radiation perceived by the human eye and defined in wavelengths ranging from four hundred to seven hundred nanometers, frequencies of 750–420 terahertz flowing between the spectrum of infrared and ultraviolet. These frequencies and light sequences are packed full of photons that move faster than the speed of sound in a straight line in and out of a vacuum.

Light is the fundamental agent for perceiving reality. It is essential for seeing the world and interacting in it. Light from the sun warms and nourishes the Earth, initiating life-affirming actions such as photosynthesis as well as providing structure for the universe. In fact, the primary tools used to probe the atomic and subatomic structures of the universe are based on photochemical reactions and light emissions.

For this reason, light transmissions of information are being used in fiber-optic telecommunication systems, lasers, and holographic technologies. These mature and emerging technologies are about to take a quantum leap in the quantum universal model of comprehending the interconnectedness of the human body with the universe. Are you ready to grasp the basics?

Photosynthesis

You may recall from elementary school that photosynthesis is the biological process converting light into usable energy. Plants make simple sugars, or glucose, and oxygen, O_2, by taking energy from the sun, using it to convert carbon dioxide from the air and ground water into essential fuel. This biological process is the foundation of cellular respiration occurring in the mitochondria of all organisms, the human body included.

Plants and animals break down simple sugars, carbon dioxide, and water, releasing energy known as adenosine triphosphate (ATP). ATP is essential for all cellular processes requiring energy. Cellular respiration, or aerobic respiration, is the series of chemical reactions that procure the reactants of sugars and oxygen, producing water and carbon dioxide by-products within the cell's powerhouse known as mitochondria. Mitochondria regulate the voltage of the cell.

In 1978 Peter Mitchell was awarded the Nobel Prize for proving enzyme complexes in electron transport occur within mitochondria, altering pH factors corresponding to thermodynamic acceptors rather than electron transport. What this means is the body's voltage is integral with the production of perfect polypeptide production for amino acids to be formed to satisfy our helices expression for regenerating the best version of ourselves. Voltage variances uncouple our helices, vary protein production, uncoupling our hydrogen bonds, resulting in deconstructed water systems and lower O_2 levels. This means our cells are not respirating properly.

Food provides information to the body for proper genetic expression to occur. Plant-based foods, ancestral foods, foods our ancestors consumed, and green, leafy foods naturally support increasing energy to fuel the body. Greens tend to house chlorophyll. Chlorophyll is imperative for photosynthesis to happen, supporting overall energy production via the conversion of sun and water. Greens are good for your health.

Another critical component is sunlight. Sunlight offers information to the body via skin absorption. The cells within our skin's dermis and epidermis house vitamin D, allowing the sun to activate D_3 conversions. D_3 is the immune-supporting vitamin D the body requires for normal detoxification, respiration, and overall repair.

Sunlight is also absorbed via the cones and rods in the eyes, allowing the body to fuel the brain with essential energy. The brain is the body's number one energy consumer, robbing from other areas to satisfy its energy requirements.

The bulk of the brain's energy is consumed at the synapses, or the tiny junctions between neurons that send and receive signals. The electrical output precedes the chemical message of said information from the electrical expression.

This ionic transference requires minerals to create the electrical charge. Minerals are imperative for polypeptide production and delivering the chemical message of the electrical output.

The gray matter of the brain uses more energy than white matter. Gray matter is made up of synapses, dendrites, and cell bodies while white matter contains bundles of axons containing large amounts of myelin or fat wrapped around the axons, insulating and preventing bioelectrical leaks. Fast signals require more energy efficiency, while watching television requires less energy in general. Heightened sensory perception such as hearing require heightened levels of acuity, therefore requiring more intense energy needs.

Unlike the body, which increases energy in times of need such as when walking or exercising, the brain consistently burns fuel. Solving difficult problems or being in a heightened state such as a soldier requires precision decisions, which require more fuel to burn. Unlike the body's ability to store fuel for times of need, the brain has no reserve for energy; therefore, it will constantly consume oxygen and fuel from its blood supply.

When neurons start shutting down from a lack of blood supply, neural connections or bioelectrical communication begins to shut down as well. The brain supports the functionality of innate body systems. Cohering the mind and body to work as one supports overall long-term wellness.

Coherence is defined as the quality of being logical and consistent in formulating a unified whole. The Heart Math Institute has been doing research into the effects of heart-brain coherence for the past twenty-five years. They have proved that heart signals significantly influence brain functions. The communication system during coherence clearly defines how the heart responds to the brain and how the brain responds to the heart.

The more stable and ordered our heart patterns, the more stable and ordered our brain patterns. Coherence reinforces positivity in our emotional and mental realms, affecting how we perceive, think, feel, and act toward life. Much like a metronome, a peaceful resting heartbeat is irregular. This natural, incoherent heart rhythm is known as heart rate variability (HRV).

HRV is proving to be a valuable indicator of overall health

and wellness based on its ability to show physiological resilience and behavior flexibility as well as biological aging. A lower HRV corresponds to increased stress on the nervous system or life-deterring cellular actions and illness. It has been determined that the main factor influencing heart variability is our feelings and emotions. Emotions directly affect our heart rhythm patterns, thus influencing our body's communication system, our light.

There are numerous studies suggesting coherence plays an important role in the excitation of energy transference of nearly 100 percent capacity, without dissipation, making biophysics an upcoming subject for fully comprehending the human's mind/body functions.

We Are Luminous Bodies

Over the past few years, people have been awakening to the fact that we are more than physiological beings living in a consumer-driven world. We are, in fact, luminous beings living in a world we cocreate.

All modern illnesses result from stress. Stress shows up in various shapes and sizes. Internal and external. Induced and experienced, prompting specific biochemical reactions known as an immune response. It presents as a community of angry, incoherent cells.

Incoherent cellular communication results in overall cellular dysfunction incapable of recycling its essence as it's been influenced by an alter response system. It mitigates inflammation, the culprit of all biological dysfunction. Looking at what causes it, we see how to deter its formulation. However, before we get into that, it's important to understand how the body functions when it's operating normally.

The body is mostly water. Water is H_2O: two hydrogen molecules attached to one oxygen molecule. These water molecules then magnetize with other water molecules to form crystalized honeycomb shapes. These shapes form geometric patterns like the patterns found throughout nature. This water structure coalesces with our imprintable bioelectrical force field linked throughout our body systems.

It acts as a battery system intricately connected to our life force. It's why we don't spill into a puddle each step we take. It's also considered a secondary system for allowing nutrients into our cells and toxins out. It correlates directly with our electrical webbing in the body known as fascia.

When we are vital, we get up in the morning and feel vibrant. We continue throughout the day feeling joyous and happy. When we encounter stress, we manage it; we do not overreact. When we get a cut, our bodies send out an immune response.

This immune response encapsulates the situation, creating a little bit of inflammation. It assesses the situation and then it pulls out tools to repair the situation. Once the repair is completed, we recycle the inflammation, sending this army of an immune response back to the barracks. We are vitally happy once more. Our cut has been repaired. We move on with our day well into the night feeling joyous, and the body runs ultraefficiently, bioelectrically fuel efficient.

Water and air are our main sources of oxygen. Water is H_2O with oxygen hosting eight electrons. Electrons offer spinning actions and variabilities, refracting energy codes via frequency modulations. Radicals are inefficient, energy drains that attract oxygen molecules.

They seek energy to proliferate, wreaking havoc when they lose electrical voltage or power.

When a radical takes one electron, we can repair it. If we lose two electrons to radicals, again, our immune response will adapt and search our bodies for tools to do a repair. We will succeed. If we lose three electrons, we have now destructured our bioelectrical force field housing information within its geometrical scaffolding, thus losing a hydrogen molecule.

Shifting H_2O to HO means we are incapable of succeeding in a simple biological repair. However, the body is resilient. It's programmed to survive; therefore, we continuously signal our immune responses to repair the situation. Each immune response generates more inflammatory chemistry, often robbing energy from other body systems to do so. This may lead to chronic inflammation and automatic body responses, locked into a chemical dependency. Chemical dependency means our bodies start seeking the dysfunction over the wellness to feel normal.

Immune System.

Everyone has an immune system made up of trillions and trillions of interactive cells. The immune system requires energy and nano molecules specifically sequenced to assure normal cell functions. These nano protein molecules or amino acids are assembled in specific order, signaling other amino acids to join in and assemble.

This structured assembly is the foundation for all biochemical assimilation. When the immune system needs help, it sends out molecules with a specific broadcast signal or frequency. The specific signal sequence is innately ordered in each cell.

The cellular communication of these specific molecules means something when they are assembled, like words in a sentence. Symptoms arrive when our cells miscommunicate, and our signals get mixed up.

This natural process of frequency molecules is essential for normal cell functions. When operating normally, it strengthens cellular communication and supports weakened cells which may have lost their voice or become confused.

Frequency molecules enhance a richer cellular defense against illness. This modern perspective of using the language of cells to enhance the immune-communication system supports immune processes naturally by targeting specific cell signals. These signals establish the health inside each of our cells, affecting our immune system along with all mind/body systems.

The immune system operates several lines of defense systems and is nourished by various systems within the body cohered with the microbiome. The microbiome is considered the conductor of the body's symphony, attuning our cells to the highest frequency for normal functions to take place.

The Microbiome and Immunity

The microbiome is made up of the digestive tract's many organisms keeping our internal environment in homeostasis. The microbiome is a delicate balance of bacteria and fungi coupled with a handful of other microbes, viruses, etc. These bugs, as they're dubbed, make up 90 percent of our body. The remaining 10 percent is made up of eukaryotic cells, or humanoid cells. The bacteria/fungi are light emitting while eukaryotic cells are light absorbing. This balance is essential for supreme immune responses.

While some people manage to maintain a strong immune function, others may in fact be unable to create the essential nutrients for maintaining perfected health. The body's self-regulating innate intelligence supports self-healing and innately fights for its survival.

When we miss a meal, don't sleep well, or get stressed out, our body's natural ability to assimilate nutrients essential for supporting our immune functions will dysfunction. This lack of nutrient ingestion or assimilation in turn corrupts immune functions that may lead to acute or even chronic autointoxication, depending on how long the body is deprived of essential nourishment.

We choose how we live and how we die. The choice to consume live foods filled with light or to choose fast foods filled with processed products impacts the quality of how we feel. The food industry is very aware of the connection between food and quality of life and spends millions to find flavors that induce cravings. These flavors are readily sold to fast food chains for profit. Our choices of how we want to feel are often mitigated by addictions implemented by corporations rather than our innate intelligence. We choose convenience while refusing to acknowledge our role in how we feel. Often these additives degrade our cellular communication, resulting in not feeling well.

Eating Our Feelings

Cellular communication is integral in lowering risk factors of poor health. Not only does food impact our communication system, but emotions also have an impact. Traumas and stress in general induce an instant derangement of the microbiome. Stress chemistry gets triggered when we feel threatened and helpless in life. While we may be able to therapeutically work through the memories and thoughts of these traumas, the fact remains chemistry is encoded within every cell of our body within our mitochondria. These chemicals are a constant reminder of our need for survival.

Stress-induced chemistries can easily get triggered for no apparent reason. A song on the radio, the waft of a scent, or a word can trigger a stress response within the body, instantly altering normal cell functions via biochemistry. This changes mood in accordance.

Trauma from the separation at birth alters the microbiome from a happy healthy gut to an unhappy, stressed-out, harmful microbiome. It's a well-known fact that trauma babies have increased inflammation in their gut. Offering short-chain fatty acid omega-3 supplementation has been proven to support normal functionality of the microbiome within a few days of a traumatic birth. Fat is integral for normal cellular communication and feeling happy and healthy in life.

Traumas like all life experiences are recycled within emotional patterns etched along bioelectrical pathways. The heart field, the biorhythmic experience of connecting deeply in vital health and happiness, gets torn. A shroud of electrical leakage consumes huge amounts of energy to hold. Long-term traumas are considered a break in the matrix of space-time. Replicated in hate crimes and the breakdown of humanity's heart. A hardening of arteries correlates with the dysfunction of a social matrix based upon falsehoods that program a competitive notion of the world.

CHAPTER 2

Body Pathways

Vascular System

Heart disease is the number one killer in the world. This hardening of the heart is the plague of our times. The past few years unleashed a fear-based rippling across the globe. Once isolated events that break down systems are showing up as catastrophes in social and economic as well as environmental issues. This onslaught of the times reminds me how important it is to innovate by comprehending the need for new ways of doing the same old same old. It's time to lighten the heart of humanity.

A conscious approach to a world recreated in an image of light. An existence of pure essence we all light up in contact with. Remaining human in nature and divine in essence. A lightening of spirit and Earth itself. A connected universal healing sounding as bells for peace resonate throughout each being. A unified tone of health and prosperity for all who choose is happening. It has already begun. Who's joining?

There are many who will preach yet few will willingly lay down their weapons of competition. Relaxing our fears and softening for life to flow lovingly and harmoniously. For all beings to feel exalted in heart and mind. A blended experience for all to partake. A feeling of being one with our very best version of ourselves. Open and flowing. Yet so many will succumb to hardened ways. Developing inconsistent light emissions is required for longevity. A good example is the hardening of arteries, our life channels of nutritional transportation.

The Hard Way

Atherosclerosis is hardening of the arteries and blood vessels. Blood vessels and arteries are naturally flexible tubes moving rhythmically with breath. These microtubes deliver oxygen and nutrient-rich blood to our tissues and cells much like fascia delivers electrical resourced information to our cells and tissues. Blood vessels are our micro pathways, and arteries are considered the macro pathway much in the same way. Micro vessels are intricate in the brain, eyes and kidneys as opposed to larger arteries supplying the outer extremities. Flexible tubulars efficiently transport nutrients to tissues for cellular regeneration and repair to naturally occur.

Atherosclerosis hardens these otherwise flexible tubes when they get a buildup of calcified toxins. Calcified buildup is often associated with poor protein assimilation and cellular dysfunction. Cellular dysfunction begins with miscommunication, varied cellular information, or incoherent light. Poor instructional insights result in being unhealthy.

Inside a healthy tube is a thin layer of cells considered the information or communication headquarters. These cells known as the endothelial cells pick up chemical communication and relay the information to the tissues and cells. The endothelial then receives insights back from the tissues and cells, altering the chemistry of the blood for pathways to receive updated intelligence downstream.

This two-way interface continuously updates the entire body system on the functionality of all tissues and cells within the whole. Having plaque buildup breaks down normal messaging and often confuses the relay system within our body systems. This in turn results in varied chemical responses and often inappropriate immune responses.

Endothelial cells get damaged by the harmful chemistry born from stress and especially animal by-products and high-saturated fat intake. A diet high in saturated fats increases LDL cholesterol or low-density lipid proteins. LDL cholesterol increases overall blood cholesterol, lining the endothelial cells within blood vessels.

LDL gets trapped and oxidizes within blood vessels, resulting in the body instigating a natural protective mode. This protection hardens blood vessels, making them ridged and prone to leakage and damage. Developing arterial plaques that calcify from calcium sticking to these plaques reduces flexibility and increases the risk of stroke, heart attack, and deep vein thrombosis. Cross sections within blood vessels get smaller and smaller, increasing the pressure of blood attempting to pass through. This is known as high blood pressure.

Plaque buildup in blood vessels deters nutrients from getting to the tissues and cells. Critical nutrients of normal functioning cells, blood sugars, and insulin levels start to increase. The increase puts people at risk for diabetes mellitus and hypoglycemia.

The real culprit of these two modern diseases is excessive saturated fat in the blood. Fat is two times the calories as protein. All cells are made up of fat. This phospholipid membrane or cell wall is known as the brain of the cell, the communication headquarters. An increase in saturated fat causes the permeability of the cell wall to also grow rigid.

A hardened cell wall hinders nutrients from entering the cell and more so for the cell to respirate and express toxins outwardly from within the cell. This critical function of essential expiration destroys normal cell functions at an alarming rate, forcing cellular voltage to reduce and overall energy to deplete.

The microbiome is the source of health, enhancing immune responsiveness through protein assimilation necessary for normal cell functions. It is also the source of all disease.

The gut is super important for immunity. The immune system is the body's defense system. It literally links cellular communication from the outer layers of our body to our internal layers via the vagal nervous system. It translates what's happening in our external realm, our emotions, and environment and how it impacts our internal messaging system through chemical variances.

The immune system is an integral messaging system throughout all body functions. It is more than just an army of defense against viruses, bacteria, or fungi. It does more than combat foreign agents. It synergistically complements all other body systems. It is in fact the foundation of all body functions to operate normally. It's where we assimilate lipids.

Harmony versus Discord

The body has several active body systems that work in harmony, keeping the body fit for life. One is the immune system, and when it isn't working properly, there're microbe imbalances inside the body. These microbes make up 90 percent of the body. We are literally a perfect balance of bacteria and fungi with a dash of viruses, bugs, and microbes. These bacteria and fungi emit light. These lights are absorbed by the 10 percent of the body that make up eukaryotic cells, or humanoid cells. This matrix of light emissions fuels our bions or the physiological aspects of our body's bioelectrical messaging system.

The microbiome is the headquarters of the entire body's communication system. It regulates communication via protein production. Protein production is essential for cellular functions. Cellular functions mitigate actions for the entire body system to achieve.

Research from the fifties and sixties shows the immune system lives just outside the lumen or tubing of the colon. This thin layer within the lumen is considered the microbiota. This is the light-emitting faction of the gut. While the immune system is primarily outside the lumen, our microbiota is inside the tube. The layer separating the two is the smallest layer of cells. These cells are permeable and influence each other. The brain gut axis of this area in the digestive tract electrically supplies the brain and organs in retaining energy efficiency. The body prefers to run fuel efficiently.

Signs of poor gut health are usually low energy, gap bloating, nausea, constipation or diarrhea, indigestion or heart burn, or a rash after eating. These are all signs that something isn't right in the gut. The goal of the immune system is to have a natural inflammatory response to ward off a cold or foreign agent without prolonged signs or recurring issues.

When our gut is functioning normally, we send out an immune response consisting of a short burst of inflammation. This acid base burns and cauterizes any threat to our health when we are well balanced. When the body is stressed or unable to produce the proper biochemistry, we continue to send out inflammatory armies to combat the threat. This prolonged immune response is the culprit of poor health.

A good example of mixed messaging in the gut is an overgrowth of candida or yeast. This is representative of people with respiratory issues. An overgrowth of bacteria or yeast skews light emissions, resulting in mixed messaging of cellular instructions. Light is information that instructs the cell on how to produce proteins to function normally.

In traditional Chinese medicine, the lungs are connected to the large intestines. The meridian system is formed via lay lines of energy connecting all body systems. When one system is deficient in energy, it will borrow from another system. This also plays out nutritionally as light is the precursor for protein and chemical production.

The gut is where the body regulates all chemistry from polyproteins essential for feeling great. One protein linked to a balanced microbiome is mano binding lectin. MBL2 is integral in regulating the bacteria fungi balance inside the gut, thus regulating the immune response. The composition of the gut instructs the entire body's internal environment.

Specific changes in MBL2 are being linked to viruses that impact the lungs as well as heart issues, kidney functions, and stroke along with numerous other autointoxication issues. It's also linked to hyperimmune responses, such as autoimmune responses, joint pain, or food sensitivities, where the body continuously sends out immune responses to restore balance. These autoresponses are considered autointoxication derivatives. Chronically, it may create a misguided autoresponse.

When the immune response is actively receiving divergent light instructions, proteins variances are presenting within the microbiome. When we are unable to squelch an immune response such as methylation, the process of converting homocysteine to methionine, we are on the verge of having a leaky gut. Homocysteine is initiated when anything comes near our mouth. It stimulates a chemical response, signaling our digestion to prepare for protein production in the gut. Methylation is essential to making our feel-good chemistry. These feel-good hormones and neurotransmitters along with all other essential proteins the body requires for normal cell functions are produced in the gut.

Current data shows that chronic diseases kill more than 41 million people annually worldwide. The entire body is made up of more microorganisms than humanoid organisms. There are more than 38 trillion microbes living within the human body, mostly made up of bacteria and fungi. The majority are the light emitters for our humanoid cells to consume. They are how we stay well and the reason we get ill. Our center of health begins with these microbes. In essence we are governed by the balance of microbiome light emersions.

Fat Supports Light

While I am not a believer in long-term supplementation, I do see the need for short-term supplementation from time to time. Supplementation is not the solution for a failing microbiome. Supporting a healthy microbiome requires eating a diet that supports normal cell functions. A balanced diet should be more than enough to stay well without the need for supplementation.

Over the past few years, fad diets have come on the market eliminating carbs or fats or mineral-based foods. The truth is we need a balanced diet of all available nutrients for the body to perform normally. While normal for one may not be normal for another, the basic nutritional needs don't vary that much from person to person. I believe the biggest misconception in our day about diet has to do with fats. Fats are essential in light transference.

A good source of healthy fats can help break down the buildup of saturated fats along cell walls while nourishing our microbiome. Good fats are omega-3 fatty acids found in nuts, seeds, and avocados. It's been known that a diet fortified in 90 percent unsaturated fats and 10 percent saturated fats supports normal cell functions for life.

Good fats are considered anti-inflammatory, neural network supporting and cellular membrane enhancing. They fuel neural expressive dendrites along the axions along our superhighway of conductivity, expressing electrical currents to synaptic receptors across calcium channels while supporting anti-inflammatory responses. Truly impressive for the body.

Short-chain fatty acids enhance immune functions and are best found in fiber. Think an apple a day keeps the doctor away. Flax meal and chia seeds are fiber sources that are also terrific for hormones. Celery and organic prunes are also easy fiber sources. Fiber is the number one nutrient found in nuts and seeds. Eating three to five servings per day of nuts and seeds is a great way to support gut health.

A high-fat diet or a Mediterranean diet that's fresh and delicious is considered globally one of the best for gut health. Health practitioners and people alike agree natural foods change our cellular functions, slowing oxidation while retaining flexibility.

Slowly making dietary changes can support longevity, fueling the body with a rainbow of colors daily, picked fresh and produced locally to infuse nutrients with local biomicrobes for ultimate cellular expressions. Food may include a wide range of colors; oranges, red beets, blueberries, greens (leafy), or yellow squashes. I love bitter greens to move toxins out of my fascia. Bitters purge toxins from the liver and bladder. They support stabilizing kidney functions along with supplying the body with much-needed minerals.

Since food is information, it orchestrates genes or places them dormant. The exchange of light supports our immune response as diminished luminosity generates disease. Food is the forefront of feeling well or feeling lousy.

Why take a supplement when nuts and seeds are readily available? Healthy fats and fiber from a mostly plant-based diet support normal cell functions prominent of long life. It's now considered the longevity diet.

Healthy fats include avocados, chia seeds, flaxseeds, hemp seeds, and walnuts offering the highest nutrient values. These nutrient-rich items are inexpensive and bioavailable to support lowering inflammation while restoring a normal microbiota within days.

Fish, while offering omega-3 fatty acids and other good nutrients such as DHA, are grown in environments that can be more detrimental to the body's immune system. Omegas in fish come from the plants they eat, so farmed fish doesn't necessarily have high levels of omega-3 fatty acids. Choose fish oils wisely as supplies are diminishing globally. Conscious consumption needs global review.

Diets including chia, hemp, and walnuts are the best source of omega-3s combined with their fiber production. The best foods to source a healthy microbiome are diets with lower levels of animal products. These menus are now considered the longevity diet across all nations.

An increase in nuts and seeds reduces heart dysfunction along with many other neolithic illnesses, including early voltage reduction due to blood sugar increases. Sugar is considered acidic in the body, causing inflammatory responses. Acidity levels alter pH. Voltage reduction reverses polarity at net zero. Reversed voltage is often emanant of cell death. Cell death happens once a downstream cascade remits missing protein patterns. This alters the light of a cell, weakening its communication.

Light emissions continue to communicate long after it leaves the cell or is transmitted. It moves along the electrical pathway lined with cholesterol. This mylar sheath offers conductivity from cell via fascia to the neural system. This fiber optic matrix connects us to everything we ingest. It serves our highest cellular expression, or it deters us from living fully by dragging us down and draining energy. This happens when we are blocked.

What's Broke Can Be Fixed

Outdated approaches to the body maintenance appear as blood variances in energy. Sugar fuels our cells for main functionality. Simple sugars are the premise of initiating communication systems. The lock and key mechanism of specific proteins coded to receive insightful information or emit instructions for cells to organize to gain a specific result is innately encoded and eternally available within our genes.

A heightened sensitivity to insulin reduces the levels of blood insulin, while conversely, higher levels of insulin in the blood increase fat storage, decreasing light aligning with the onset of risk for tumor growth. A lower secretion of insulin increases our life span as it encourages light emissions to exchange for best results.

Insulin, an anabolic hormone, stimulates growth more than any other hormone, testosterone, or human growth hormone (HGH) included. Insulin promotes growth. When tissues block the uptake of insulin, we fail to stay lean. We insulate our tissues with fatty acids, a sign our cellular uptake of insulin is blocked. When our tissues are blocked, we tend to form a padding of adipose tissue. Adipose is stored fat for later energy consumption.

This fundamental layer of obesity in our youth culture is indicative of an onset of illness. Increased adipose means the liver's muscles, tissues, and organs are incapable of normal function. They're no longer protected from insulin. In turn, blood sugars spike, cascading into a plethora of other energy leaks plaguing our cultures.

Body fat surrounds cells so insulin is unable to work to get blood sugar out of the blood and into the cell where it's required. Electrical pathways are nonproductive, alluding to a blockage. Blockages are often emotionally housed, embedded within the cellular matrix as a restraint.

We are undoubtedly a community of trillions of cells organized in harmony. Living together cohabiting as a being, in community with other beings on the planet. We thrive in like-minded, like-hearted environments that support our creative expressions. In essence, we are light, not heavy dense beings isolated from connection. Density is the ignorance in forgetting our innate nature is light. Pure and simple.

To be clear, I am not alluding to a misconception that people who weigh more are heavy, ignorant, or dense. I know many people in the world who are light who weigh in over a couple hundred pounds. Density refers to the lack of light emissions within the cellular matrix of the form they reside in. Lightness requires fluidity within the matrix of the body. Adipose blocks fluidity.

Fat stagnates our connectivity unless it's good fat. Adipose induced fat slows us down. Moisture conducts electricity, while tissue tightness harnesses a drain on the bioelectrical system. Adipose-produced, meshlike tissue is inconducive for elevated electrical conductivity, by natural law.

Inflexibility is the first lesson I learned in yoga. Balance was the first I learned in psychology. So many lessons to teach on how angiogenesis, or fat storage, increases during cellular replication, altering beta cell production essential in controlling glucose levels. A nutritarian diet decreases the need for insulin, thus promoting normal cellular energy requirements for normal chemical and physiological systems to harmonize. This offers flexibility and balance to all systems—mind and body.

Low-carb eaters do not have lower blood sugars. A diverse diet aimed at regenerating a healthy microbiome is the best answer for restoring normal cell functions and a valued quality of life. Live food supports our life for life.

Food is light. Various sequential components produce nutrients rich for our senses and entire body systems. Light is the precursor to feeling vibrantly alive and healthy. Light instructs each cell, tissue, and organ how to regain and maintain normal functions. When the light sequence is off, our cellular communication is skewed, leading to altered protein production and possibly bioelectrical variances that in turn downregulate genetic expression, resulting in long-term energy decline. Energy decline results in cellular stress, stress-induced swelling, or puffiness may at times feel warm to touch. These aches and pains are plaguing the many seeking help within our current health organizations.

Teaching that the body is bioelectrical has never been more crucial in education, raising awareness of the potentiality within humanity as a whole. A group conglomerate, and alignment of heart and soul. A divine design aligning our heart and mind.

Physiologically speaking, healing occurs when chemical reactions, the core of all metabolic actions in the body, release energy. This energy releasing or exothermic comes into balance with the endothermic or energy-absorbing responses.

Energy sourced from chemicals influence how a cell performs, respirates, expirates, and regenerates. Biochemical reactions of electrical signals drive cellular communication and functions. Aligning our natural state expands our awareness of our higher self, our innate intelligence, our source awareness.

The Body's Electromagnetic

Modern medicine recognizes life requires a heartbeat. The heart is the first organ to develop during pregnancy and is critical for providing oxygen and nutrients to the developing embryo. The heartbeat is widely used in current diagnostic analysis. Heart rates and rhythms along with brain activity are at the core of modern diagnostics.

Doctors rely on heartbeats to identify deeper issues within the body. Electrical activity is a precursor to all biochemical and physiological actions. Therefore, vital signs are checked at the onset of most any and every medical appointment.

The magnetic field is an organizing field keeping matter in place. All organs in the body generate their own magnetic field with the heart and the brain emitting the largest measurable fields to date. Low-frequency magnetic fields induce circulating currents within the body's field. These patterns coalesce with the field on the planet, driving behaviors as well as physiological changes in the body as well as socially and economically. To sum it up, we are biochemical electromagnetic beings made of source energy realized in form, sharing the experience with 7 billion other human beings on planet Earth.

The notion of an electrical or magnetic biofield connecting all of life with the universe has been around for centuries. Paracelsus, Isaac Newton, and even Albert Einstein all alluded to the notion of a governing force regulating all life. Quantum physics has proved we are connected to the field, to the universal source of life.

New scientific evidence in quantum physics is contradicting old ways of looking at the universe and ultimately the world we live in, including the body we animate in the world. Changes in the life field or biofield correlate with shifts in voltage present, prior to illness, as well as changes in mental states, personally and collectively.

CHAPTER 3

Basic Needs

Maslow alluded to the basic needs of human beings to thrive. Food, water, air, warmth, and care were the basics.

O_2

Oxygen offers the environment essential for normal energy levels to be present. Amino acids provide the essential nourishment our cells require for regenerative proliferation. Water is a critical element necessary for elimination as well as electron transference, and light is derived from all aspects of life.

Oxygen is critical for life. Most of us get our O_2 simply from breathing. We know we can't live without it. But did you know that the world's O_2 levels are decreasing? Science shows the body requires 19.5 percent O_2 from air to replicate perfect cells via hemoglobin conduction for vital energy and longevity to occur. The current global atmospheric status of O_2 in most major cities and suburbs is approximately 19 percent. This means that unless we are drinking ultrapure hydrogen structured water or doing vigorous exercises, chances are we aren't getting our daily oxygen requirements. This is showing up as increases in cognitive and breath-related diseases permeate our culture.

Oxygen is probably the most important element for cellular regeneration since it offers superior electron transference supporting chemical bonding and reactions to take place. This means the foods we ingest convert into usable forms essential for replicating perfect cells, enhancing immune functions, and keeping us energized easier when our O_2 levels are optimal.

O_2 is essential for keeping peak brain functions. Low O_2 levels are responsible for lowering mitochondrial stimulation (due to decreased electron exchange) lowering cellular energy or ATP output, resulting in neurological and cognitive decline. This means neural networks require a higher cerebral blood pressure to maintain ultimate brain functions.

Most people who exhibit signs of high and sometimes low blood pressure are often oxygen deficient. Atherosclerosis or hardening of the arteries is associated with neural death or apoptosis of a shrinking brain's decreased metabolic demand, resulting in low oxygen levels and higher risks for stroke. In other words, oxygen is essential for cognitive functions.

One of the best ways to deter cognitive decline is to drink more purified water. We all know we're mostly water. Water is H_2O. H_2O supports our bioelectrical battery system. O_2 is the main element that keeps our energy consistently charged. It's also a catalyst for all biochemistry to occur. When we're deficient in O_2, that shifts our hydrogen molecules, uncoupling our electrical circuits, supporting the accumulation of hydrogen bonded heavy metals.

This uncoupling also supports free radicals that we know are damaging to all body systems causing premature cell death and biological aging. Years of research have led me to find natural ways to restructure our body systems using natural O_2 enhancers, such as deep breathing, exercise, and tech devices. These do-it-yourself techniques and technologies allow us to take charge of our body's environmental oxygen requirements. How are you supplying your brain with the vital nutrients it needs?

H_2O

Structured hydrogen water is a perfect solution for eliminating toxins from the body's cells. It deliciously supports our electrical systems, making it easier to assimilate nutrients while improving cellular elimination. Smaller molecules are why structured hydrogen water enhances our bioelectrical field. Smaller molecules are easily absorbed, generating fuel efficiency.

Neutrigeneomically speaking, the body has been considered a protein-producing machine, when functioning normally, using carbohydrates to fuel cells, proteins to repair and regenerate cells, and lipids or fats to repair and regenerate our fiber optic, bioelectrical communication system, our neural network. Thanks to quantum physics and biophysics, we recognize the body is sourced in light. Light is the fundamental agent required for life to present.

When we feel good, we wake up, spring out of bed, and feel amazing while driving to work. We don't get angry if someone cuts us off on the road. We are well balanced. We flow through the day happily and return home happy to share with our friends and family.

When the body is off kilter, we find it difficult to get up in the morning. We get angry when a car cuts us off. We complain about work and find it difficult to focus. We are cranky when we arrive home, and our wounds don't heal as readily. This is a sign of being imbalanced.

Clients seek me out to feel better, sleep better, have thicker stronger hair, get rid of constipation and bloating, lose weight, get pregnant, and generally feel happier. Experiencing any signs of energy deficiency is a sign of cellular dysfunction and protein inconsistency.

You see, the body has very specific requirements to operate. When we have these elements available, the body feels amazing, we're happy, and we look awesome. Others can sense how elated we feel, and we attract good things into our lives. The same is true when we don't have the proper pieces. That's when we start feeling tired, rundown, and cranky. These are signs that we are out of balance.

The body is designed to regenerate through homeostasis. A give-and-take duality if you will. We inhale and exhale. Intake and eliminate. Generate energy and expend energy. Move and rest. All while retaining perfect balance. When there is a sign of imbalance showing up in our life, then our body is not achieving homeostasis.

A balanced life starts with recognizing what holds our attention. Ask if its life affirming and constructively supporting us living a fulfilled life of our dreams, or are we wasting time and effort zoning into a game console or gadget of sorts, mindlessly letting time slip by? Sedentary lifestyles are known to produce lower dopamine levels, notorious for sadness and depression to set in.

Inactivity also propagates sluggish digestion and circulation, resulting in many medical conditions of the twenty-first century. Issues with blood sugar and lipid levels are two of the leading causes of death in the United States. While these numbers rise, the sale of virtual gaming systems and large-screen TVs is also rising.

I'm not saying we need to go out and run a marathon or walk a ten-minute mile. I am saying that not moving will reduce your life expectancy. The longer we sit immobile, the more likely we are to die prematurely. Lifestyle is comparable to how we live and how we die.

DNA: Our Innate Blueprint

The modern health movement has discovered that health is a cooperative communication of many genes expressing in unison. This polygenomic communication is a symphony of sorts, a frequency individualized for each human being. Our frequency signature is indicative of our innate essence of self. When we are attuned, we feel great! When we are experiencing dissonance, our body's chemistry is off-kilter, and our bioavailable energy is depleted. Resetting biochemical balance requires our polygenomic broadcast signal system to communicate efficiently.

Divinely designed from pure molecules, our bodies are specifically blended to support the broadcast signal of genes respectfully controlling the expression of vitality. These sequence-specific signals, when varied, cascade to disrupt other signals, resulting in 99 percent of common ailments.

There's a handful of base genes that harmonize the perfected broadcast signal of the polygenomic factors in replicating perfect body functions. By enhancing the natural broadcast signal of these specific genes, we attune pitch-perfect harmony supporting protein proliferation of healthy cells for emerging vibrancy.

Identifying deficiencies within the body allows us to consider what foods we can incorporate to adapt our energy back to normal levels, achieving efficient protein production and utilization. While most who exhibit signs of energy deficiency are protein deficient, it is essential in understanding where in the body the protein deficiency stems from. If it is coming from the inability to eliminate, it's a specific deficiency pathway. Bloating or having a rash after eating is again a different pathway causing the deficiency.

Every person has their own blueprint of the proteins they require to feel their best, which is why there is no one size fits all in helping people feel better. Isolating specific nutrients essential for each organ correlating with specific stress points along neural pathways is personal and different for everyone.

The neural pathways are considered the superhighway of the body, connecting the brain to the body and each cell to the next cell. That means trillions upon trillions upon trillions of connections continuously sharing information.

This super information highway requires very specific minerals to relay the signal that carries the information instructing cells on which proteins to produce. While some proteins require alkaline minerals, others require acid-based minerals. What this means is to reset the body back to normal cell functions, we need to specifically identify where the body is energy and protein deficient.

Nutritional Stressors

Once we isolate protein deficiencies, it's easy to see what foods and combinations will realign the microbiome back to homeostasis. The microbiome is the digestive system. It stems from the mouth down to the anus. It is filled with sphincters that open and close, allowing foods to move from one area to the next. Each area is responsible for specific digestion and separation of foods ingested, turning them into necessary proteins our body requires at that specific moment in time.

When we eat, food comes into the stomach where it is met with hydrochloric acid, melting its contents and moving them into a cooling tank known as the duodenum. In the duodenum, the first layer of fat is used for instant energy to ensure the body is recycling the hydrochloric acid until needed again. The fuel from this layer also supports the production line of amino acids being made downstream in the digestive tract, supporting our cells' energy needs.

The small intestine is a protein-making conveyer belt of sorts where polypeptide proteins are strung together based on the genetic expressions of cells signaling a need for replenishment. The body delivers these nutrients via alveoli lining the digestive tract to the bloodstream. This process of assimilation is one line in making proteins our body requires for sustaining normal energy levels.

Once the body delivers the essential base proteins to the cells, entering the cell becomes the next phase. I've witnessed many clients with candida or parasitic activity on the outside of their cells blocking assimilation of delivered nutrients, altering cellular functions, and eventually depleting cellular voltage. This is another phase to review in assessing the body for energy deficiencies.

The more deficient our cells are operating, the more likely they are to alter the harmonics of our genetic expression. This is often the reasoning for any energy decline. Voltage is the output of energy. Cellular voltage is greatly affected by the output of genetic expressions.

DNA is found in each of our 100 trillion cells containing the blueprint of our whole, like a holograph. DNA contains the instruction manual for our body system and life to operate supremely. Everything about us physically and spiritually—the features we have, such as our eyes, skin, and hair color, as well as our personality and disposition in life—is encoded within our DNA. Even our soul's purpose is encoded within our DNA.

DNA Revisited

Traditional genetics shows us that nucleic acids form the letters of our genetic language. Groups of three codons are akin to root words. There're sixty-four total root words in our genetic language. There are sentences and paragraphs containing thousands of grouped words written in our gene codes.

There are twenty axons that build proteins intrinsic for our body with a mere four codons starting and stopping transcriptional replication. Less than 1 percent of our genetic matrix has been identified in genetic research of the past sixty years.

The remaining 99 percent, once discarded as junk DNA, contains the light coding codons. These codons are considered noncoding DNA by current standards. This 99 percent of our DNA uses high levels of energy to preserve and repair itself. If it weren't important, our innate intelligence wouldn't work incessantly to preserve its integrity. There is evidence that this segment of DNA is responsible for the distinguishable human traits governing which genes get expressed and which remain dormant.

A few years back, I gifted my family with DNA test kits for

Christmas, thinking it would be a fun way to see who we are and how we are connected throughout the world.

Out of the tests we did, mine was the only one that had variances not shown in the others. My sister and father showed what we already knew: we are European with trace amounts of Eastern European. However, while my DNA results showed this to be true, my main DNA expressing in me comes from Asia, with the majority coming from India. It was remarkable to see how my DNA traveled literally across Europe, through Asia via Mongolia and Pakistan, into Indonesia, and across the sea into Colombia and Peru. Clearly my expression is different from my European-looking family members.

This is because within noncoding DNA sequences are areas prone to establish regenerative properties by triggering the expression of early growth response (EGR). EGR is a master of sorts, regulating other gene expressions essential for regeneration. This gene regulates other genes downstream, allowing them to stay dormant or express depending on the necessity of correlation for regeneration. EGR is the circuit breaker part of our bioelectrical matrix. While the circuit of EGR is similar in all humans, the wiring connecting the circuitry is different based on epigenetics.

New understanding of this piece of the puzzle is leading to research on how to regenerate limbs and organs. The full potential of our DNA component is interconnected with the epigenetic or environmental factor regulating which genes get expressed and which ones remain dormant. There are layers upon layers of electrical circuitry among the coding and noncoding areas of DNA that correspond with the overall biocircuitry underlying the entire process of our genetic expression.

CHAPTER 4

Old Meets New

Most people view DNA from a side view perspective resembling a slightly twisted ladder of our double helix. When we choose to look down at the top of the ladder, we see a different image. We see a geometric pattern known as the flower of life.

DNA houses self-charging scalar energy and is continuously sharing energy to regenerate and replicate via a geometric pattern known as the flower of life. DNA circuits harmonize light emissions or frequencies to maintain DNA integrity. These specific light sequences dance along the rungs of the ladder, in specific order.

This precise circuitry directs which molecules will be taken from the various rungs along the ladder and assembled into proteins. When the proper proteins are presented to the cell and the cell assimilates them into the cytoplasm of the cell, they get destructured. This breakdown goes further by transferring light emissions from nutritional pieces into various other elements, all instructed by the light of our chromosomes lining the ladder. The low-level light emitted from our DNA is coined biophotons.

The Light of Our Cells

Biophotons were publicly called so by Fritz Popp in the 1970s. I remember reading my parents' weekly magazine featuring string theory. I became fascinated that we were all connected in some way to the universe. This made perfect sense to me as I naturally could feel and see colors on people vividly. However, while string theory has failed to be proven, it has led to an increase of a vast amount of evidence of a unified field.

String theory led me to seek more insights into the universal connection between things. While visiting family in Europe, I came across a magazine article discussing the light of life discovered by Fritz Popp. This was a major turning point in my life at age nine, I became compelled to learn as much as I could about how we are all connected through this light.

Popp proved the body and all living matter constantly emit and receive a low-level coherent light known as biophotons. This low-level light in my opinion is the light of God that resonates through each of us. This light communicates to other cells and tissues via the universal field, gathering information and adapting to the physical body as necessary.

During the 1930's & 1940's, Wilhelm Reich alluded to a universal light that connected all of life as well. He claimed the body has a certain amount of this light, which he called orgone, that is derived from bions. When we are happy, our orgone is ignited, and when we are saddened, our orgone levels drop.

Reich was imprisoned for stating that all people needed to do to feel better and heal their body was to change their mind and generate more orgone. He said sharing love was a wonderful way to generate our vital life force. He died in prison for claiming we could feel better by raising our energy levels. He wasn't wrong.

Reich's theory of orgone and its conscious cosmic origins have been proven over the past few decades, thanks to several orgone organizations. We now know that bions, the light of our cells as Reich coined them, are what Popp considered biophotons. This light emission is our life force with the sun being the greatest emitter. Solar energy gets embedded in our molecules, allowing new microorganisms to formulate. Light supports life.

We've also discovered that orgone is mass free, it's etheric and omnipresent, and it's a medium for electromagnetic and gravitational phenomena to take place in the quantum arena. Orgone is dynamic and in constant motion within the field, exhibiting a fluidity in motion. Orgone is attracted to itself, thus merging into life structures. There is much evidence of the underlying presence of life born from this energy source found at orgone.org.

So, if feeling good means we regenerate and replicate healthy structures of life, then how do we generate more good feelings? This is the quandary of our time. When we say be more loving or make love not war, what is it that allows us to express a truly loving feeling? And for all purposes, let's not confuse making love with sex. Love is pure heart while sex is often physical without any heart, let alone a pure heart connection. A lack of conscious connection often leads to unwanted pregnancies, hurt feelings as well as painful truths about our physical connectivity when it ends.

Making love, when based in conscious expression, generates life-giving energy, the essential life force. Ancient teachings passed down from many different cultures offer insights into how to harness this life-giving energy. Meditation and breathing are great tools.

Especially since DNA changes from being tightly bound into a relaxed state via meditation. Love begins within the self and is not the result of being coupled with another. It is the realization that we are all connected and when conscious, we choose to show care and concern for ourselves and others.

Meditation and deep breathing cohere our body, oxygenating and relaxing our mind and body into a state of coherence without the need of a partner. This is where our 99 percent or noncoding DNA gets activated. This section of DNA regenerates and replenishes our biophotons, or bions, and our central communication center.

Bions are present within the body as well as absorbed via light-sourced violet light from the sun. Einstein's paper on a heuristic viewpoint concerning the production and transformation of light explained the characteristics of frequency, not necessarily intensity, observed at 0.1 hertz. We know this frequency to be the sweet spot of the Earth's frequency as well as our essential heart rate variability.

Since the 1990s, the United States has been placing more importance on the bioelectrical spectrum of cells in medicine by developing a few technologies supporting its detection and recalibration. Lasers are one tool in this arena. However, other countries, including Russia, South Korea, and Germany, have been utilizing these evidence-based, peer-reviewed technologies for over a hundred years. Much of the data received by these studies has not been shared with the US. Isn't it time we took a new look at how the body utilizes light to fuel regeneration as well as disease?

Energy Stores in the Body

Muscles are considered battery packs stacking upon each other like batteries in a flashlight. Movement charges these batteries, allowing other areas of the body to receive electron transference. We understand sitting for prolonged periods of time decreases cellular voltage.

Sedentary lifestyles whereby one is sitting for breakfast, sitting in a car going to work, sitting at a desk, sitting at home in front of a television, and then lying down to sleep deters the body from recharging. Movement is the number one means of recharging muscles to full capacity. While lifting weights can help with body strength, yoga and gentle movements are probably the best to utilize full energy capacities since they offer the opportunity to move mindfully with one breath one movement.

Outdoor activities in nature are best for enhancing overall energy, not only for the purity of oxygen levels but also for the negative ions received from natural settings. Negative ions tend to relax the mind and body matrixes, allowing the body to calm and restore normal functions. Silence is another way to reduce the electron drainage of overactive thought processes.

Light Emission Pathways

During the 1960s, the highest level of photon emissions was detected from plants published by Konev et al., appearing in "Luminescence of Various Organisms." This paper outlined the various intensities of bacteria, fungi, insects, and vertebrates.

Published in 1969 in Europe's *Biophysics* magazine, it proved that ultraweak photon emissions are a widespread natural phenomenon.

In humans, light from the cell is transferred via fascia. Fascia is a superhighway connecting every cell, tissue, and organ lined with neural connections, making it sensitive to stimuli. This inner scaffolding is the body's internal infrastructure of electrical and physiological aspects. Fascia has four main parts interconnected that keep our inner workings intact. The structural, intersectoral, visceral, and spinal fascia are flexible and supple components that constantly pump in a gliding action, moving nutrients and toxins via consistent blood flow.

Fascia is the webbing of our bioelectrical system rhythmically sustaining motion when functioning for our highest good. It connects all cells, tissues, and organs through fibers made up of collagen. Collagen is $COA_{2.}$ This fiber optic system allows the body to communicate effortlessly across the internal and external surfaces. COA_2 bioelectricity conducts best when the body is amply hydrated with plumply spinning oxygen molecules in place fueling integration.

Bioelectric circuits are based on chemical and transcriptional networks with ionic expressions regulating cellular behavior from an epigenetic control. These bioelectric signals loop within the body in close range as well as long-range, thus shifting voltage capacities of ion flows and electric fields. Modulating these bioelectrical signals controls cellular proliferation and regeneration.

Bioelectricity regulates cells, tissues, and organs by initiating chemical responses to occur. The chemical signals are picked up along the bioelectrical communication system made up of fascia and neural networks, allowing ionic channels to fluctuate, controlling the communication pathways while controlling chemical pathways. These biophysical forces regulate cellular behaviors.

Blending Biophysics

Biophysics is crucial to understanding voltage or hydrogen potential in the body. Cells work in balanced communities or frequency groups signaling interventional and developmental variances, regenerating and reprogramming indicative of desired outcomes necessary to achieve homeostasis.

When the body is low on energy or we are feeling less than par, our body may not have the ability to produce proper proteins essential to the task at hand. This in turn results in less than par results in repairing and regenerating.

The body will continue to do its best using what is available to correct itself. This often results in lower hydrogen potential, lower energy, and weakened cellular communication. When we don't have the right voltage, our signals are weakened.

Cell collectives with lower signal expressions result in stagnation due to less light traveling into surrounding tissues. This stagnation is often the onset of cellular breakdown and modern-day illness. It often is initiated by a rundown feeling. Tuning into the body and recognizing what the body is relaying back to us supports taking a break and resting, eating nutrients that are filled with light, moving, meditating, and telling our body to recover.

Mind over Matter

A few years back, I encountered a client with a severe parasitic infection. I realize it was destroying their microbiome and protein assimilation. It took me several weeks to witness the onslaught of energy decline. My client went from being a vibrant athlete to an anorexic, barely able to walk, feeble person.

The initial treatment offered by the medical community moved millions of parasites invading their digestive tract into their body and tissues. These critters were literally jumping off them every step they took. I was mortified to see critters on my table after our initial treatment.

Their initial insight to visit a doctor failed them miserably. That's when they took matters into their own hands. I went to work to clear these parasites from their entire body system. I taught them how to use intentions and meditation to rebuild the body system that was deteriorating rapidly.

The one thing that made the difference in their recovery was moving into a meditative state of being who they wanted to be. As soon as they employed this attitude of gratitude for restored health, their life began getting back on track. Embodying what it felt like to move, dance, and feel amazing is when they had a major breakthrough.

I helped them grasp that meditating on being who they wanted to be, feel, and experience reset the cellular matrix to remember who they are. It took several months for their body to catch up as is the case with energy moving at the speed of light or faster and reality or density taking time to manifest.

The greatest lesson I learned during the experience was how

incredibly resilient we truly are. I have been blessed with good health most of my adult life. As a sickly child, I learned how to harness my healing powers through meditation and nutritional combinations by age sixteen.

Helping others regain their energy and lifestyle has humbled me tremendously. We all go through a health crisis at one stage in life or another. Regaining voltage often requires help. It's OK to ask for help when we need it. Not one person has all the answers even though we are connected to source. Sometimes we need to have a different perspective on how to act upon our insights.

In short, my practice has taught me a great deal of respect for the bioelectrical states determined by ion channel expression and functions of fascia. Fascia carries the charge to surrounding cells, causing the ion channel to open and the positive ion to enter the cell. These ions alter protein production within the cell, initiating gene expressions.

These modulating growth factors of intracellular signaling and feedback loops of pH regulate regeneration via stem cell activation. The ion channels regulate proteins downstream and cascades of cellular communication essential in restoring homeostasis, influencing cell membranes, modulating signals, and regulating volume and voltage while altering biophoton expressions of DNA.

DNA's ability to regenerate protein production for longevity and youthful resilience stems from its ability to express normally. DNA expression happens when the helixes are loosely bound around the histones. Histones carry the light codes or information of our codons, specific to the language of our body's innate intelligence. The more conscious we grow, the more adapt our light becomes.

This shows up in geometric patterns of cohesion within our genetic matrix.

Until recently, this knowledge was considered sacred and shared only within secret ordered societies passed down person to person. The human genome project along with the discovery of quantum physics is merging this knowledge base with science, sharing it with the entire global community.

It's known that DNA is sequence specific, with very specific frequencies organized in a harmonic symphony generating homeostasis. However, not everyone has the same music within themselves. Each person has their own song that is unique to themselves. While each organ and system require similar nutrients for every person on the planet, the processes each person takes to generate homeostasis are slightly different based on their epigenetics.

Epigenetics is the one factor governing genomic expression by supporting relaxed states of loosened helixes that allow expressions or conversely restricting expressions by tightly bound histones around the codon. The expression of genes is controlled by how we feel and how we react to the world at large. This means we control our genes.

Reprogramming genes requires an internal coherence. Homeostasis is the coherence of our internal state, and when we are out of balance, our internal state needs to be reset. Some people can access coherence via meditation. Others may require technology such as Heart Math's heart variability device known as the EM Wave. Others still may require the assistance of a trained practitioner in energy or frequency healing modalities. Whatever the case, everyone can reprogram their DNA for health while achieving coherence.

Incoherent states promote long-term variances in genetic expression that are passed down through generations. This means if our body is chronically stiff and tight, blocking our genetic expression of flexibility, then chances are our children and their children and their children to come will have similar variances.

This was prevalent during the genetic testing era where people were discovering they were MTFHR variant. While anyone can reset their methylation process, many were sold supplements by less than ethical companies and individuals who truly believed it was the only way. I am here to remind you all "I Am." I Am refers to being one with our divine creator, our universal source, our highest self.

CHAPTER 5

The Light of Life

When we choose to be that which we seek, we become that. Expressions follow our impressions. We become what we believe. When we accept, we are powerful beings; we choose to live in our highest truth. We become our best version of our healthiest self.

Our DNA is a blueprint carrying the innate code of the universe within it. Our core essence is the expression of this code made into form. We are all expressing our divine essence in life. Some of us are in the stars, while others are looking at the stars. I don't mean movie stars here. I'm saying we are all able to master the human body and alleviate ailments and the preprogrammed notion of deteriorating as we mature. We are all able to live an extraordinary life. Living in our highest consciousness, supporting all life to flourish in kind.

When ill, the healing body requires intervention at the level of the energy body. Bodily or physical intervention alone often results in a recurrence of the illness. We see this in most ailments today whereby medical solutions require continuous use to keep symptoms at bay.

Clearing the energetic blueprint imbedded within is the only way to prolong purity of a cell's life expression. Recognizing our energy body is an organized coherent cellular matrix formulated into a community of body systems known as our body beautiful is essential.

Working with the energy body, we see most ailments are embedded in early childhood programs of hurts and pains. These traumas and hurts are locked into the energy field, altering the energy frequency of chakras and meridians. It takes a tremendous amount of energy to store old wounds. This energy must come from somewhere; often it is syphoned from stronger organ systems. The more we borrow energy from other organ systems, the less coherent our body systems are. This leads to low energy, depleting nutritional support for organs. Energy healing goes to the source of the energy leak and resets energetic pathways through intentional coherence while clearing old patterns once stored.

The Age of Healing

Healing works on the whole of a person. A mind/body connectivity must take place; otherwise, there is room for illness to return. Balancing mind/body allows our energy field to expand, taking the shape of a torus where energy fluctuates up the legs from the Earth and out of the head in all directions, connecting us to the universal field. This orblike field contains our entire energy field from birth until present. Current instruments can see a minute image of this field. While seeing it doesn't make a person whole, feeling connected to it does.

Learning to see and feel within our energy body, we become connected to all of life. This awareness breaks down any barriers between us and them. It unites us into one another and all beings large and small. Respectfully honoring this other as our highest self supports a mutual reception of integrity and upliftment.

The culture we've been taught to believe—in which we compete and generate dramas filled with toxic emotions that spill into generational dysfunctions of unconscious living and dying—is being rewritten. Revitalizing the wounded, those with blocked energy and emotions, begins with clearing our own hurts and tuning into our own personal energy field. Once we accept who we are as human beings, we can help others see who they truly are.

Right human relations require us to take a deep look at our core essence. What is our intention in our actions? Why do we want to connect with others? To what means are we seeking our higher self? I've witnessed immeasurable inhumane acts against children, women, men, and animals. I cannot condone actions that shred the life force of another in any way. Egoic states tend to present as acts against living beings that rightfully do harm. These malicious acts against others fail to cohere humanity; in truth, they deter human longevity.

Clearing humanity's imprint begins with each being clearing our own personal imprint. When we don't heal from these hurts, they become the core relationships we experience with different people. The same scenario replicates over again until we figure out how to move it out of our energy field. Failing to clear these stagnant energies, we unknowingly attract supporting actors that allow us to live the pattern again and again.

Unhealed traumas organize in our energy field that is connected to humanity's energy field and the universal energy field. We are constantly cocreating reality with every other human on the planet.

The level of dysfunctional hurts we each carry is the source of the current state of the world.

Our traumatic energy patterns are like electrically charged fingerprints that carry a charge equivalent to our original hurt. When a specific imprint of our wound is triggered for whatever reason, the explosive response zaps our chakra systems, shrinking our energy field. Habitual dramatic stressors from childhood traumas where we don't feel safe show up in 99 percent of illness I've helped relieve.

Early childhood and intrauterine hurts make up most energy patterns plaguing our world. These imprints are the blueprints of generations of pain requiring mass healing for humanity to move forward as light beings. How we experience life imprints our energy field. Isn't it time we start teaching our children about energy and human potential?

When we harness the power of energy, we formulate patterns in the luminous energy field, clearing imprints that cause illness prior to illness manifesting. Our genetic blueprint aside from the physical and chemical pieces houses the energy unit of our divine matrix. Changing our bodies by changing our interaction with the field helps the world be a healthier place. When we choose to keep life as the same old same old, we choose to allow illness to manifest and people to continue disrespecting one another via violent acts that disempower humanity.

There is no other being who can dream your dream. The level of life experience we choose to accept is limited only by our imagination. Our desire to live a better life springs from a will to live life to its fullest. This desire is inherently programmed into our limbic brain as a survival mechanism that goes dormant when we allow too many gadgets to distract us.

Buying into a program, believing we need that new car, or that new something or other to feel happy. Allowing ourselves to be programmed as mass consumers means we give up our personal freedoms and allow others to tell us what to dream, feel and experience. We allow their dreams to become our reality. Your dream is your dream. Never give up on your dream.

The Chakra System

Chakras are wheels of light akin to glands for specific organs in our biosystem. These funnellike vortexes adhere to the spinal column extending funnel wide outwardly. They act as energy receptors, infusing energy from the field into our neuro sensory system via our glands, directly correlated with the function of said gland. Each gland supplements an organ by secreting specific hormones in correlation with the biochemical imprint of that organ. Glands are akin to gas stations to fuel up on electrical conductivity via a biochemical signature.

There are seven vertical chakras running along the spinal column within the body, with the eighth connecting the top of the head outwardly to the crown and a ninth completely free floating in the energy field of the luminous body connecting to the universe. As information is received, physioneural connections trigger stored information in our body systems, opening us up to manifest a specific outcome. When our electrical biosystems are purified, we gain healthful results. If there are blocks, we get skewed results, repeating these outcomes until the impurities get cleared.

These wheels of light spectrums are indicative of us being in the body, not the body. The body corresponds to the thoughts we harbor and what we place in our bodies. This means we are responsible for how we feel and should be mindful of what we place in our bodies, the thoughts we keep, the nourishment in ingest, drink, and consume, as well as the company we choose to keep. Chakra colors are innately set for optimal attunement via natural flow through the spine.

Chakras host innate intelligence within frequency patterns resonating in harmony. Alternating harmonics alternates experiences. Light and sound are considered waves at length. The precision of experience is intense. Perfectly tuned in pitch. Imprinted and stitched. Light flows in rhythmic patterns. When we feel well, we are balanced. When depleted of energy, we are off kilter. Choosing to raise our frequency by altering our choices in what we consume and with whom is our given right. We all deserve to feel good.

Chakras offer a first line of defense against the onset of negative results. It offers a sensory perception of what is on the horizon, a gut feeling, a divine attunement, a grounded instrument finely tuned for the best possible outcome. Balancing chakras supports balancing our internal and external realms.

The Meridian System

The meridian system is another bioenergy information system running through the body back and front, up and down. This superhighway connects our organ systems via specific pathways and identifying points. The points correspond with our organs, plexus along the spine, and identify energy or chi variances. The meridian system is the main energy system utilized by traditional Chinese medicine, acupuncture, Shiatsu, and emotional freedom technique.

Chi energy runs along twelve main meridians that are partnered in energy and nutritional exchange. This shared community allows the body to borrow energy from one organ system to support another during times of need. Imbalances or blocks in meridians tend to drain corresponding organ systems by robbing essential energy and nutrients essential for normal functions to take place. This in turn cascades into energy and nutritional deficiencies resulting in illness.

Meridians are part of the light-infused information system of the body. They are considered a means of tracking the body's subtle communication system. A road map of the bioelectrical system connecting every cell, tissue, and organ to its fullest potential. Unlike fascia, meridians are very specific indicators of energy variances presenting in organ functions. These bioelectrical potentials available to our body systems are generated by biological processes measured in millivolts.

In general, light fractures into six colors: purple, blue, green, yellow, orange, and red. Meridians are lines of light set in specific frequencies. Consider the light emissions of the meridians like the light from the sun shining outwardly in spectrums of color. While we do not visibly see the various colors from the sun, the fact that these frequencies are present is the same as how meridians hold light frequencies.

Frequency expresses itself as bands of light. If frequency surrounds us, then it is within us. It applies to the universe as well as within our body systems. This subtle energy is considered fractal. Scaling from small to large. Einstein knew all things begin from a thought. From thought, we create a blueprint of how to attain the thing we thought of. A means of achieving the thought. Meridians work in a similar fashion by taking thoughts and the electromagnetic energy of the emotion connected to the thought and transforming it into the blueprint for our body to take action to express it as matter.

Meridians are living organisms adaptable to change and resilient, capable of avoiding illness and recovering from it. There are twelve main meridian systems with two additional meridians that support these twelve, including the stomach, spleen, heart, small intestine, large intestine, lung, kidney, bladder, pericardium, triple heater, liver, gallbladder along with the two that intersect these called governing and conception meridians running up the front and back of the body. These lines are planes of energy connecting the body to the field.

While many people consider a meridian to represent the state of a specific organ, this is not necessarily true. Someone with low kidney chi may have a lung variance as one meridian nourishes another. A qualified acupuncturist or Shiatsu practitioner will be able to identify the variances necessary for restoring normal energy patterns. These energetic patterns originate in the field and are activated via thought processes and emotional or electromagnetic signatures attached to these thoughts.

The planes of energy of these bioelectrical pathways show a geometric precision within the body. The sequence-specific electron emissions correlate with our innate harmonic convergence in mass. These moving energy systems charged by currency support a depth of health innately within everybody, expressing physical wellness. Thus, fractal geometry formulates the physical constitution of our body systems. The geometric patterns connect planes of energy the same way as we see in the quantum universe. The body is also filled with these fractal patterns connecting us to everything.

Fractal patterns repeat in nature and in the body with a section of the body being a representation of the whole. Think reflexology with the foot housing the energy pattern of the entire body. The foot in this instance mirrors the whole body, with areas of the foot representing aspects of the organs within the body. Modern medicine is beginning to respect this insight. For instance, fractals show us how to read the pulse or temperature in different areas of the body.

Restoring health using fractal insights bridges the subconscious mind with the conscious mind. The world of physics teaches us to connect to the zero point or 0.1 hertz, connecting us to the unknown source energy, connecting our subconscious with conscious mind. Pattern thinking infuses the healing artist to see the body in new ways. An example is seeing the nervous system as frequency. Geometry is the pattern of the invisible frequency into physiological patterns appearing within interior systems and how they support overall wholeness. This vantage point instills how we are all connected and how each person can accelerate our ability to heal not only ourselves but the world we share.

Grasping the seen with the unseen energy patterns requires courage to accept there is an innate source of life ordering the best version of wholeness for all to enjoy. This understanding is rooted in ancient teachings, some that are synthesized in religions, but more so, rooted in thriving cultures within history. The geometry of the body respectfully is part of the greater whole as all frequency moves together. Energy, if you recall, does not dissipate; it merely changes form.

Consider meridians like dermatomes, or areas of the skin used by Western medicine in identifying a specific nerve plexus associated with the specific area of the body. The nerves are connected to the spinal column and are considered a road map for neural variances along the spinal column. Meridians are the invisible light pathways connecting the entire body and its systems. Variances in energy are easily recalibrated via restoring meridian pathways for normal cellular communication and chemical communication to occur within specific areas of the body.

Westerners are beginning to accept biophysics as a viable tool in comprehending modern illness. The fact that electrical impulses initiate physiological shifts stems from ancient Eastern philosophies of wellness blending into the future of medicine. Teaching our children these very basic fundamentals of how the universe and the body are energetic expressions formed in matter is how we overturn the current burden on health care and assist humanity into a greater level of life worthy of our species.

SECTION 2

CHAPTER 6

A Purified Heart

There is more than enough evidence proving heart variability resonates as peaceful, life-affirming experiences. Teaching resilience and heart variability techniques ensures we as a community of global citizens achieve a harmonious world for generations to come. Recent science exposed the photonic expression of a resting heart releases an average of forty photons per second. In contrast, a heart filled with joy expresses more than 100,000 photons per second. Living joyously clearly amplifies our light.

The Heart Wants What It Wants

Why? Why has the death wish grown into such a plague in society? Even before the pandemic embraced Earth's mindset, a wish to leave this plane has taken over the light force in many. Just look at the increase in drug and alcohol abuse. In Western society, the overabundance of obesity and disease plague our health-care system. Mental health issues and the lack of movement among people have grown disproportionately with a desire to love life.

What causes a death wish? What mitigates a desire to leave the confines of the body? To escape physical reality via addiction to technologies, food, sex, or mind-altering substances. What if everyone who chose to suffer chose eternal happiness instead? An immortality from physical and mental confines.

History is marked with fads. Exercise, fitness, sexual provocations, hedonism as well as philosophical alignments of immortality. What we believe to be real is real. Imagine what the world would look like if everyone decided to be fully responsible for their part in creating a reality filled with respectful, happy, healthy beings. What would that look like? How would it feel? Why wouldn't we want to experience that?

We are at a pivotal time in life whereby science has proven our emotions change our chemistry and our chemistry changes the quality of our life. Our inner environment is more important to our health than our external environment. Our relationship to ourselves and to our body is determined by the quality of the experiences we have in our perceived reality. The competitive world is not a viable way to live eternally. It is unnatural to create harmony and global cohesion when people fail to cooperate. In fact, nature is by nature cooperative and will gladly support our needs when we choose to work within the natural rhythms and cycles presented.

Ancient cultures recognized this for centuries, until man came to tell them that their way wasn't the best way. The best way for whom? For commercial business? For egocentrics who have been wreaking havoc on humanity for thousands of years? When ego takes the lead, we lose heart, compassion, and our connection to humanity's highest potential.

There is a reason why the heart is the first organ in the body to develop. We hear the heartbeat of an infant in the womb before we fully grasp its features. The real mystery of the heart is what triggers the heartbeat to begin. What sparks the heart into the rhythm of life? How do we ignite the beginning of life? Something triggers the body to life. Something larger than life. Something larger and life affirming with more creative power than anything else on the planet generates this spark of life into existence.

It is within this spark of life that we can regenerate an entire body system, allowing the body to grow, heal, and regenerate a new form. This spark of life continues to regenerate and repair the body during life, for life, and is best nourished with the proper environment. The physical environment thrives with fresh air, sunshine, and purity of water and food, while the inner environment is resilient in the company of kind thoughts, feelings, and emotions.

There is absolutely no doubt that stressful thoughts generate stress chemicals that break down the body quickly, dissecting fundamental proteins required for repair and regeneration, often leading to disease. Stress chemistries are best managed in brief periods since they are not sustainable for life. Carrying stress results in holding weight and decreased immune responses. Unresolved stress is diabolically dangerous for propagating disease.

Changing one's perspective is one way of disconnecting from a stressful situation, allowing time to review and resolve the issues in a less stressful way. Another way is to breathe. Taking a deep breath in and slowly exhaling. This prolonged breath offers time to pause and detach from a stressful situation. Stress is a major culprit of disease and mortality. A simple breath can help us live longer by giving us pause to see things differently.

People often wonder how a thought can change chemistry in

the body. Thoughts trigger emotions that form a reaction known as a feeling. These feelings promote a chemical reaction in the brain. The chemistry of the brain either supports life and life-affirming cellular actions within the body or it deters life-affirming actions by shutting down processors with stress chemistry.

Emotions can be a response to a current situation or from a memory of the past or the projection of a future event. The brain is incapable of deciphering the time frame of the emotion; it only responds in kind with a correlating chemical reaction.

Heart variability is gaining acceptance as a major factor in long-term health and happiness. The little brain or neurites in the heart outmeasure the number of neurites within the brain, proving the heart is critical in producing and relaying essential electrical and chemicals components for the brain and body to function. Our ability to self-regulate propagates life-affirming chemistry measurable from the heart. Heart variability is only recently considered a marker for longevity.

Western medicine is based on a trend that is continuously being proved outdated. It claims that the body cannot be helped unless it receives outside support. New science as well as the science of homeopathy and ayurveda support the fact that the body heals when the internal environment supports life-affirming actions.

So how do we get to a place where the internal environment is harmonized for ongoing wellness? The place where the body is on autopilot deterring the deterioration process known as aging? To fully grasp this concept, we need to collectively change our perspective on what we think being human is.

Old Shifts to New

Schools and universities have been teaching for more than a hundred years that humans are derived from animals, specifically chimpanzees. This is questionable. Archaeologists agree that humans are their own species who lived along Neanderthals on the planet for thousands of years.

We are distinct via our ECG or electrocardiograph, our genetics, and our chromosome 2, which appears to be genetically fused for heightened intelligence to pursue. These distinctions offer humans the capacity to consciously feel and choose our actions. These are two factors that make humans undeniably distinct from animal lineage. It is literally impossible we came from chimps.

Humans haven't changed for thousands of years. Humans discovered across the planet in tombs and caves dating back thousands of years are the same as humans today. We have not changed significantly enough to support Darwin's theory of the strongest surviving. Our distinct chromosomal mutation hasn't altered one iota since the first human set forth on the planet.

Chromosome 2 is what empowers humans to have the conscious ability to choose. It is prominent in humans but not in other species we supposably evolved from. It is the one factor offering conscious choice of longevity over decay.

DNA, the underlying blueprint of life's essential requirements for human existence, is directly correlated to the internal environment we keep. Epigenetic studies show how genes regulate essential protein production for normal cell functions.

To be clear, genes express or digress into dormancy. Normal cell functions generate life-affirming actions within the body such as a supreme immune system with high-functioning regenerative properties including the production of longevity polypeptides.

Think about it. When scientists perform an experiment in a laboratory where they place cells or organisms into a petri dish, they monitor the behavior of said specimen. When the specimen responds in a manner that concludes life-affirming actions the environment is considered supportive. When the specimen responds in a life-deterring mannerism, the environment is considered toxic.

The entire body is a giant walking petri dish. We are either supporting its proliferation of vitality or deterring it via toxic environmental factors. The choice is evident in our beliefs, the thoughts we keep, our emotional response to life in general as well as all we choose to ingest.

Basically, we are designed to heal and regenerate. If we are exposed to healing concepts rather than blindly led to consuming a pill for recovery, then true healing can happen. True healing is available for every individual, community, country, and global inhabitant. The genetic blueprint is not hard coded. It's a preset genetic code influenced by choices and the thoughts filtered from those choices. These are the activators of our gene codes. These epigenetic factors include and are not limited to love, compassion, nutrition, how we respond to life, coupled with the childhood programs we are inherently running unconsciously.

Activating gene codes responsible for regeneration and repair requires sparking the appropriate frequency. Because light and sound are waves and particles, the tones we use when we speak, the frequency of the foods we eat, the purity of the water we drink, and the attention we allow our minds to hold all support normal or abnormal genetic expressions. Epigenetics influences our gene codes through our beliefs and environmental choices.

Changing our environment, we change our genetic expression, even if we were born with variances of expression. The only factors we are unable to resolve as humans are additional genes, such as those found in Down syndrome and other rare genetic disorders. While not everyone can shift into perfect health overnight, everyone has the potential within them to accomplish vitality in a short period of time once they make necessary changes to how they choose to live. Change our energy and we change our reality.

All choices impact the binding of DNA around histones within the chromosome within every cell of our being. Activating dormant areas is accomplished by relaxing these bound areas of DNA. This is how we access epigenetic controllers regulating our genetic expression found in our noncoding segment of DNA.

The noncoding region is essential for establishing homeostasis of sequence specific harmonics of innate biophoton emissions. These distinct coherent patterns are rooted in the innate language of life. Exact sequences of light encoded as language modulate regeneration via a continuous connection to the quantum field.

Changing How We Feel

Thanks to quantum physics, separation of body and energy does not exist. It's known to be one in the same. This insight is based on the placebo effect. The placebo effect is believing in recovery by taking a sugar pill with the belief that it is a new type of drug that will cure any ailment. The placebo effect proves the belief heals, not necessarily the pill itself. This concludes that positive thoughts control cellular biology of recovery.

Equally important is the reverse-engineered model of thoughts. Negative thoughts are detrimental to cellular recovery. Thoughts are exceptionally powerful in shaping life. The nocebo effect is the fact that negative thinking can cause any ailment to occur and even kill someone if they believe. Think of a man who is given a three-month life span based upon lab results read by his doctor. The man died three months from that valuation. That is how powerful the mind is.

I worked with a colleague who lectures internationally. His doctor's office called to remind him to have his labs drawn for his upcoming appointment. He was scheduled to fly out that evening for a weekend convention but agreed to have the labs drawn before his flight.

Jack, not his real name, had a very busy day in his practice, and while he intended to leave the office precisely at two to get to the lab prior to his flight, he was met with unexpected circumstances. This led him to leave the office at two thirty, around the same time most schools let out. This in turn kept Jack tied up in traffic until he arrived at the doctor's office for his lab draw with less than an hour to get across town to the airport. Jack had to wait in line and eventually got his labs drawn just prior to three forty-five.

Jack barely made his flight, went to the convention, and upon return the following week, received a distressed call from his doctor asking him to come into the office that day. Jack complied and learned from the lab results he had a brain tumor. Jack couldn't believe the labs were that precise in showing a malignant brain tumor; however, his doctor was convinced the critical values appearing in his blood were conclusive of a very fast-growing brain tumor.

Jack was stunned. He hadn't felt ill. No headaches, no vision loss. Nothing out of the norm. Jack, a well-established natural medical doctor, asked for a redraw of his blood. While he fully respected his physician as a colleague and friend, he couldn't accept this diagnosis. Reluctant to redraw and wait for the results, Jack's doctor agreed to a redraw.

Jack's labs came back the next day showing Jack's blood counts were in their normal range. So, what led Jack's doctor to conclude that Jack had a fast-growing terminal brain tumor in the first place? Well, remember Jack's original labs were drawn on a day where he was crunched for time. That crunch led Jack to produce high levels of stress hormones, to the point where his body was creating the perfect environment for a terminal brain tumor to manifest.

Jack's environment nearly led him to have radical brain surgery. That's how powerful we are and how detrimental stress hormones are to the body and its regenerative properties.

Recognizing thoughts are not just passing fleeting ideas; they are proven physically and biologically to generate life experiences. Thoughts vary our cellular matrix, not our genes. Genes will remain intact no matter what our thoughts. However, thoughts will dictate if they express or downregulate.

Thoughts generate feelings, and feelings generate biochemical expressions. Genes are blueprints like a builder uses. There is no turning on or off. A builder reads the blueprint to build what they are building. Consciousness is the architect guiding the builder gene. The body is under epigenetic control, not genetic control.

Epi means above the genes, which means the mind is controlling the genes based on beliefs and consciousness. How we've been programmed and what we believe control our genes. This awareness means changing our consciousness, changes our body's health. The fact that stress is the cause of disease correlates with the need to shift from stress to relaxation.

The Heart and Head

The advanced human bioelectrical magnetic system can be accessed and regulated on demand, based on the choices we make in life. How we act, feel, and respond initiates our beliefs. These are responsible for the emotional choices we make in response to what life brings our way.

Achieving a goal of vitality can be difficult or easy. Realizing we already have it generates an electrical signature into the field, promoting its presence to occur. Once we learn to respond to hurts and disappointments in a new way, we can change our chemistry in our body and propagate changes in the experiences in our life. Traumas tend to get locked in on a deep tissue level within the body system and may require deeper work. (Resources are available at the end of the book)

Reacting to what may have looked like a failure in the past can translate into life-affirming chemistry based on an attitude of gratitude rather than a victimhood state of mind. An attitude of gratitude allows healing to take place by seeing a difficult situation from a different view.

This healing process is an ongoing process that harmonizes within the body's systems and seamlessly regenerates the body, despite the chronological number we may be. It doesn't matter how long the reactive pattern has been in place; we can shift it into the now and change a failure or hurt into a powerful, positive experience, changing our life into more fulfilling experiences in the process.

For years I've worked with challenged children in inner-city schools offering mindful movement and breath techniques. These simple techniques offer tools for us to disengage from external factors that are drawing us into being less than vibrantly alive. These simple techniques teach us how to harness our inner being, remaining calm while chaos is around us while amplifying our light capacity. Literally people light up when we get into a cohered loving state. We glow.

This technique is widely taught to the military, police, and athletes as basic training to maintain composure during stressful situations. Remaining nonreactive has proven to save lives while framing outcomes into the most beneficial experience for all involved.

How can it be that something inside the body can have an effect outside the body? The moment we ask for something in prayer, we affirm it is beyond us. Feeling it, embracing the emotion of having it right here and right now, supports manifesting it in the here and now. To think it creates it. To feel it is to manifest it in the likeness of that feeling. Thinking stressful thoughts replicates stressful situations. Feeling beneficial thoughts, even during difficult circumstances, can shift the outcome to benevolence.

Repeating Patterns

During the late 1800s, a spiritual revolution merged with a scientific revolution in a shared vision that changed with World War I and World War II. The wars diverted humanity's attention from spiritual awakening and scientific emergence by focusing the global mindset on competition. A similar spiritual revolution is taking place today, right here and right now. Will we continue to choose to compete for the limited resources, or will we finally learn that we are all in this together? One global community learning to share what is available for life to exist on the planet.

During the pause of the past year and a half, humanity at large had an opportunity to delve deeper into meditation, prayer, and spiritual expansion, yet many choose to divert their attention away from the inner realm to seek solace outside themselves via mindless technological gadgets. These gadgets tend to harness our internal energy systems, slowing down our healing process and programming the mind with overstimulation that may result in long-term neurological disorders. Disconnecting from the inner realm of peacefulness deters life.

The world is facing the mass extinction of not only animal, plant, and insect species; people are exiting at an alarming rate as well. I've been volunteering at a medical facility keeping an eye on the pandemic outcomes in our community. While we had large numbers of people leaving the planet during the pandemic, the numbers have continued as adults are experiencing postpandemic issues and children are exiting at an increased rate.

Speaking with colleagues who are witnessing the same, it is known that the energy or frequency of the planet is shifting as the old is merging with the new and the newer energies are uncomfortable for many. Many are exiting because the world is not the arena for their growth currently. The old way of doing things no longer serves the young and the choice to exit is being taken. This is also showing up in the increase in suicides among young people as well as veterans.

This in no means condones suicide or a death wish. The death wish has come to an end. A thriving time for flourished environs has already birthed anew on the planet of life everlasting. Waking up to our part in the coherence of 0.1 hertz is where attention is needed. An experiment worthy of review. A prognosis of sorts with eyes wide open. Curiosities got the better of me. Indulge in a section of humanity's nectar and decide which way humans should grow.

CHAPTER 7

Can I Get a Witness?

Humans are considered superior beings on the planet by most people who reside here. In truth we are only a reflection of a greater source of creative genius. When we are in a dark room without a witness, no one sees our genius. It takes a witness to experience our greatness. How great a people have we become?

We're All Connected

The late 1800s birthed a famous experiment proving quantum physics, changing how the world views reality. Fast forward one hundred years to fully reveal the impact it had on social awareness. The experiment is of course Michelson/Morley verifying a field of energy connects everything in the world.

Initially, the experiment failed miserably, due to the fact it was performed inappropriately, restricted by the knowledge base of the time. Similarly, Darwin's once thought to be true theory of evolution no longer holds true. The unified field was discovered in 1987 by repeating the original experiment with updated instrumentation, thus proving the outside and inside of the body are connected to everything in the universe.

Similarly, the power of prayer proves healing thoughts can be helpful to someone around the world, via quantum entanglement. When a family friend was diagnosed with bone cancer, I remember each night before going to bed I would intentionally send myself to her bedside to breathe in life and breathe out the harmful effects of the radiation and chemo treatments she was undergoing. I was a kid at the time and thought these dream states were just because I was unhappy; she was ill.

After a few weeks of nightly visits, my father called her across the Atlantic to see how she was feeling, and she asked to speak with me. During our conversation, she asked if I had come to visit her during the night because she awoke to find me sitting by her bed with a glowing light around me. I was astonished she had experienced my intentions so vividly, as if they were real. I now understand they were real. We can share our healing with others no matter how near or far. Human beings are that powerful!

Our family friend recovered from bone marrow cancer, and her less than 3 percent chance of survival has been deemed a miraculous healing. For us, it was just the way it was supposed to be. Our friend chose life after our conversation. She decided she was no longer going to let cancer rule her experience. She chose to kick cancer in the butt, and she did! Her mindset changed her outcome.

So how did my intentions help our friend feel better? Nicholas Geyser formulated when two photons are used to increase excitation (when he tickled them) they respond in kind at the same time. My intentions of supporting our friend's healing were integrated with my precise energy directives to purify her body with each breath she and I shared.

While I used my mind to voluntarily execute my will, she was connected to the field and became aware of the nurturing taking place. This supported her recovery, whether she was aware of my intentions or not. We are that powerful. Little did I realize as a kid what I was doing or how incredibly potent my will could be.

Engaging one's heart, the strongest electrical and magnetic field in the human body, has a greater magnitude than the human brain. When we harmonize the heart and brain, we access a coherent state that's optimized in 0.1 HZ. This happens to be the frequency that dolphins and whales use to communicate throughout the world's water systems. Apparently, it's also the innate frequency of the planet.

When we feel feelings in the heart, the brain responds in kind. When we feel coherent, our brain connects and amplifies the emotion that ripples throughout the field, reflecting the state of grace back to us through our experiences.

These coherent techniques of healing have been documented throughout human history for thousands of years. How we apply it in our lives can co-create a healthier, more cooperative community. The current global community is changing rapidly. A merging of science and nature is required to fully incorporate the principles understood by our ancestors. Science now recognized our world is one of integrative electrical and magnetic fields. This is an accepted fact.

The Power of Breath

Ever notice how somedays we find we flow through life effortlessly, enjoying heighted states of grace and true happiness, while other times we are reactionary in a spiral of never-ending glitches that stop us from moving forward on task? Sometimes it seems like we make mountains out of molehills. Or we realize, *My God, how did I get here?*

Focusing on the heart, we move out of the mind. Infusing feelings of gratitude, we emit 0.1 HZ to the field. Try it. Sit and close your eyes. Find your breath. Feel free to place one hand on your heart and one on your belly. Notice what you notice. After a few deep, soft, rhythmic breaths, find something, anything, that feels happy, grateful, joyous. The feeling can be from a memory, a future possibility, or the now.

Simply breathe. Breathe in the feeling of joy. Breathe it into the heart. Allow the outbreath to emit joy from the heart outwardly, surrounding the body in an orb of frequency. Feel free to add a color to the energy orb or simply breathe in and breathe out. Notice the difference in how you feel.

This fast coherence technique is a powerful tool in resetting our gracious state and may be used anywhere for any length of time. For a more intense experience, consider the following:

Sit, preferably with an erect spine, relaxed and comfortable. Take a deep, cleansing breath in through the nose and out through the mouth. Repeat these two more times. Now regulate your breath. Breathe in for a count of four, pause for a count of two, exhale for a count of four, and then pause for a count of two. Repeat. Maintain this rhythmic breath throughout the practice. The more we practice the longer we can hold this state of grace.

Breathe in gratitude; breathe out gratitude. Draw the attention to the heart. Shift awareness to the heart center. Feel the feelings of joyous gratitude. Come back to the heart when the mind tries to interrupt. This is the space of heart/brain coherence. The state where deep intuition resides. A place of pure creation.

This is where our innate intelligence guides us to our highest possible potential. When we embrace living our full potential, we fully engage universal consciousness. It just takes practice. Repeat often. Commit!

Mind/Body Connection

The body mirrors our beliefs. What we believe about ourselves and our experiences in the world manifests within us. When we see ourselves as healthy, vibrant beings, we choose to be healthy, vibrant beings. When we tell ourselves that at this or that age, we'll have aches or pains, then rest assured, we will have the aches and pains as soon as we gain that target number.

The sad part is that most everyone's daily thoughts are completely unconscious. The mind runs on a gambit of beliefs instilled as a child through our parents' beliefs and from those we were surrounded by before age seven. This is awesome if we are surrounded by genius creatives who are highly conscious. The brain of a child is in a hypnogenic state, meaning it absorbs patterns from those around us.

The experiences we have during young adulthood and adulthood are the mirrored beliefs we picked up along the way. Heart/brain coherence is a fantastic tool in undoing the beliefs we habitually have been mirroring in our bodies. It is a highly effective tool that is simple to practice.

Embracing each moment with a choice of gratitude is a direct reflection of what we harbor within our body. Every disease, hurt, and pain is a portal into our body, reflecting energetically the belief we are holding. It shows up as a mirror reflection when we criticize other people's choices as well as our own.

Our thoughts communicate with every cell in the body. The body houses more than 100 trillion cells. Each cell is extremely social and communicates within the communities of other cells. This is how we can speak directly to our body to heal or unconsciously communicate disease through choices of life-deterring actions toward ourselves or others. The heart broadcasts our feelings no matter what the aim.

From the heart, an instant knowing takes place to affirm our life or to deter its growth factor. The one thing that can make an instant change for life to blossom is perspective. It is impossible to activate life-deterring parts in the brain when life-affirming areas are engaged. We cannot be happy and angry at the same time. We always choose how we prefer to feel. Yes, it is that easy!

Changing our mind, and practicing being mindful of the thoughts we choose to keep, may initially feel uncomfortable. It may not appear to be having an impact, then one day our entire perspective will be aligned with life-affirming experiences if that is truly what we choose. In other words, it takes practice and dedication to stick to that practice.

The Picture of Health

Specific gene expressions may correlate with illness, but they aren't responsible for illness. We master our genes and have the power to override any ailment eliminating the need for relying on health care to continuously fix us. This in turn resolves the burden on our outdated health-care model.

The US model especially is a business model that pays exceptionally well so there is very little incentive to consider an alternative. However, while volunteering at an emergency room, I saw firsthand the understaffed facilities attempting to manage the onslaught of a pandemic.

We lost more than half our nursing staff due to the conditions. As a member of the international nursing association for more than a decade, I can honestly say our health-care system is crumbling without real solutions. The acquisition and management of health-care facilities are operating from an outdated model based on the bottom line.

People must choose to realize we are our own healers. Taking responsibility for how we look, and feel is a sure way to start a shift. Releasing outdated concepts such as Darwinian theory and accepting that we modulate our gene expressions is critical to share with our children.

Acknowledging Darwinian theory of human evolution as a series of accidents in genetics is inaccurate information we continue to share. This realization alone will rapidly help shift consciousness on the planet. *Why* humans are here is never answered by Darwin. I'm not a biologist; however, when I look at how life blends and adapts, I see a garden of life. A glorious world of cooperation where organisms adapt to their environment.

Nature Nurtures

I lived on a mountain a good part of my life without television or electronic distractions. This led me to feel at one with my environment. I developed intimate relationships with the animals in my neighborhood. Living in a large city, I continue to emit a frequency where animals on land and sky feel comfortable enough to come visit, sit near, and bring their young. Cocreating a cooperative habitat within the garden for all to thrive.

The natural world is a literal garden that humans reside in. Sadly, the natural world is in peril. Humans are tasked at being the conscious guardians of this magnificent planet. Yet we've allowed our sense of purpose and obligation to get distorted. Human history is filled with destructive patterns that continuously repeat. We allow empires to be built only to be destroyed. What if we chose to do things differently?

We are at a stage in history on the brink of what's considered the sixth mass extinction of life on the planet. This virtual reality depicts the decimation of people, animals, plants, rivers, and soils. The scene precedes human consciousness in recognizing we are symbiotic to these elements for life. We are sorting through what aligns and what no longer serves overall life on the planet.

CHAPTER 8

A Long and Winding Road

Life is a series of actions we take to receive desired results.

The Collective

The ugliness of humanity's collective is coming to the surface. Humanity's collective consciousness must find a way to remove these splinters and recreate a viable solution for all to thrive in. Remember we are a global community. Cohering global consciousness allows all life-forms to prosper.

There is a reason why the planet houses each species of plant, insect, animal, and such. We are all pieces of the whole. By removing one element, we alter the livelihood of the remaining elements. We are currently on the verge of depleting more than one-third of the species on our planet. How much loss do we need to experience before we realize how valuable each species on the planet is to our overall well-being?

Consider the microbiome and the many different organisms necessary for it to provide proper nourishment for our body to thrive effortlessly, fuel efficiently. The various species coincide with the variety of our internal and external surfaces. What if humans were resonating in a harmonic field indicative of other species being present for harmonized perfection? An orchestrated symphony of the stars requiring all life to tune in?

We versus Me

I recall standing up for issues as a young adult, pleading with Wall Street types to encourage their awareness that the Brazilian rainforest was indicative of the lungs on the planet. I worked diligently to raise awareness of preserving the balance of nature on the planet.

During the eighties, I also shared how clean water is imperative for sustaining life and how large beverage corporations should be denied access to the rivers in India and Africa to bottle their products and produce wastewater for the downstream villages to consume. These companies literally take water away from the desperate and dying, generating mass amounts of plastic waste while turning a profit.

The new science discoveries offer clean drinking water options that do no harm and ways to clean our wastewater, so the rivers and streams are not harmed requires an awareness of the harmful practices that convenience has on our environment. First and foremost is shipping. Continuing to use trees or plastics devastates the environment, especially when enhancing the consumption of fossil fuels used to transport. Chemicals in the land need to stop. The land can only take so much.

Technology that pulls water from the air may be reviewed

along with methods to clean up human wastewater. These are just a few ideas that get sparked when like-minded, like-hearted beings collaborate.

Businesses are encouraged to review how many nonrecyclable plastics are produced in one year. How many trees do online shopping platform consume so they can ship packages anywhere in the world. Rethinking how group mentality continues to destroy the resources on the planet is essential for sustaining life so we can have an immediate gratification of convenience. When did we get our ideals mixed up?

Food, water, and land are all sustained for humanity to conscientiously enjoy for eons is gifted when we continue to experience conscious living. Conscious living starts at 0.1 hertz.

Consciousness requires us to reevaluate every aspect of our lives. Every connection we make, every product we endorse. Chances are if people knew the fast foods they consumed burned rainforests to produce the palm oils to cook their fries, harming animals lives, would they really choose that fast food? If consumers learned the top brand shoe's they're paying a hundred-plus dollars for are made by enslaved children, would they insist on wearing those shoes?

I guess the adage "Ignorance is bliss" holds true for most. Awareness comes at a cost. It holds people accountable for their actions. It raises the bar on what we will tolerate from others and demands respect for all. "Black Lives Matter" equates to all life matters. Your life. My life. The elephants' and whales', and the trees. All life is precious and deserves respect. We receive what we give from what I understand.

I continue to advocate for these issues by using my buying power to vote for the lifestyle I prefer to support. The richest people in the world generate the most waste. Space debris, destruction of the Amazon rainforest, and rocket fuels pollute the air and waters of every inch of our planet. Does being rich give humans a right to destroy humankind for personal power?

How have we as a collective allowed this to be our conscious norm? To excite in the thrill of online shopping for convenience while our neighborhood mom-and-pop stores close and our communities crumble? All for the sake of one or two men to have it all. Really? This is the dream people are choosing to live.

Life as We Know It

Life has been eliminated five times on the planet, and I am sad to report humans are on the same trajectory at this time. Life is thriving, yet human consumption is driving human extinction by disconnecting us from nature.

We are meant to live in harmony in the garden of Earth. We have chosen to live out of harmony out of cooperation with nature by choosing a competitive perspective. We are competing with nature rather than cherishing it as a part of our very core being.

This disconnect results in the imbalance we are facing today. A world where people are disconnected from conscious acts and programmed by technologies that are dehumanizing them at a faster rate than ever before.

I've lived without television for many years, yet during the past few years, I started watching television shows or movies on Netflix. These shows impacted how I felt the next day since I was watching mainly at night. When I would wake in the morning, I found my thoughts resulted from the experience I encountered the night before.

The stress level hormones would kick in and my mood would be different from if I did yoga the evening before. The effect of the television wasn't in my highest interest. It was a plug-in to drain my energy and keep me from being my highest self. My innate connection to source was impacted by choosing to watch a program instead.

There's a reason why televisions, video games, and computers have programs. They draw our attention in and program us out of our natural human state into a dependent state of stimuli from outside sources. This is showing up in the increased health issues people are experiencing. Think about it. Especially when the mind overrides the body and vice versa from habitual patterns of our subconscious.

Lasting changes take practice and discipline. Identifying the scaffolding of what it feels like to experience the element we think we are missing equates to most as a feeling of loving acceptance, lathered in respect and care for the entire being of each other. There's a human conglomerate unfolding in a heart-based coherence.

A fine-tuned awareness of what works and what no longer works for our coherence requires changing our belief system. This is critical to turn the world into the garden it is intended to be. Humans are the caregivers of a world where all people can be considered equal, and all beings live a life worth living in health, peace, and harmony. This message has been passed down throughout the ages in many ancient texts, throughout many ancient religions, yet has been buried by people seeking to control the masses for personal gain.

The ego-driven control of humankind transforms from the

power of a few to the power of the masses with the expansion of human consciousness. Who is with me in creating a world where children, their children, their children, and so forth have a natural world to play and experience wonder in? Understanding that life is not a struggle and evolution is not based on the competition of a struggle.

The current winner/loser model of the world accepts that starving people are less worthy than Westerners who own a big house and car. Humans creating mass extinction is not natural. Recognizing all people are worthy and connected to one another instills a value as caregivers of the natural world. We are all cocreating by allowing inclusive creativity or destructive separation. Cooperation is the driver; instilling new beliefs of human potential is paramount.

Taking responsibility for our actions, consciously growing aware by recognizing what signals we're producing in our thoughts, which chemical signature is running our body and consequently generating our reality. Ultimately, we innately recognize incoherent actions prior to taking them and choose to align with light-affirming actions that produce life-affirming results for life to flourish.

Teach Our Children Well

The brain is the most complex computer in the world. Having no programs or APs on the computer is a result of education. Education is in dire need of review. Programs are integral to running our computer.

The central operating system of the brain is turned on during the last trimester of gestation. Programs we accumulate after birth are based on observations we make about the world around us.

What we encounter from birth until seven is the foundation of our programs used to live from.

These programs are downloaded whether they are based on kindness or in a not so loving state. Conscientiousness respectfully comprehends the attunement of 0.1 hertz. Benevolent beings enfolded in heart-based mastery, no longer afraid of what might be, embracing the knowing of what is and shall ever be.

The frequency of a childlike brain in a hypnotic state is programmed via theta brain waves, the state of imagination. Theta brain states run from three months to approximately age seven and program the unconscious mind. These programs are downloaded as behaviors via observation. Think monkey see, monkey do. After age seven, the programs become hard wired in our operating system and are the basis of how we respond to life for life.

We begin operating based on how the people around us operated. The programs are locked in as behaviors based on how those around us felt, acted, and responded to life. When the outcome is hostile, the operating system is magnetically drawn to thieves or discordant rants that propagate disharmony. The operating system resides in the subconscious.

A conscious vessel is creative. It can operate from a wonderful place in the world or from a dismal space. Consciousness looks within to access answers. The subconscious mind will override the thinking brain when consciousness is operating. The subconscious runs the operating system 95 percent of the time. Growing mindful is critical in reprograming the subconscious mind.

Moving from Me to We

To shift global awareness, we must recognize the inaccuracies we've been taught regarding genes controlling our characteristics. We must also recognize that the environmental connection of the nervous system is consistent to a harmonic score. The more advanced the harmonic nervous system is, the greater consciousness is available. This is in direct proportion to the exchange of light sequencing of communication through the field into body systems.

Consciousness communicates via cell receptors along cell membranes, transmitting it to effectors that take light sequencing information into the system to adapt its biology. The receptors' effector proteins are the fundamental units of consciousness transferred into perceptions. Minimal cell membrane results in minimal consciousness.

Human beings are a growing conscious community where like-minded beings come together, generating a global conscious community. Operating as one unified cooperative cellular body and team of humanity

Understanding advancing evolution for ourselves and our species is available to everyone. Shifting from human to humanity requires a breakdown of the current structure similarly to a caterpillar transforming into a butterfly.

Consuming nutrition in the form of a plant prior to moving into a chrysalis, the caterpillar emerges as a butterfly. A completely new and different organism from when it cocooned. Gossamer wings acting as solar panels absorbing light, allow the emergence of a newly developed light being.

Humanity is currently in the caterpillar's destruction mode.

Breaking down its structures that no longer serve a sustainable way of living. Civilization's voracious appetite, consuming everything available, is reorganizing into a light aspect of being. An evolved heart-based species of conscious beings.

If our current system doesn't consciously break down, it will self-destruct. Times are a-changing and the best possible outcome for humanity is available to proceed past the failures known to history. We all have a vital role to play in growing conscious and applying our heart-based creations for our planetary garden to flourish.

Heightening awareness of our unconscious actions is necessary to realize a new paradigm for humanity. Unconsciousness can be experienced while thinking deeply during an afternoon drive or through a sudden surge of emotions rising to the surface. Awareness brings a lightness of being, joyously engaged in heart-written ways no longer a dream of the grandmothers' way. We act humanely towards others. We transcend lowly ways. That day starts today.

CHAPTER 9

It's All Energy

Irrefutable evidence proves we live in an energy world. Everything is made up of energy. Energy is the scaffolding for matter to present.

Energy to the First

All energy originates from source via frequency patterns in density of matter. Changing our emotional responses changes our energy. Harnessing higher levels of energy promotes a positive impact on our surroundings instilling a desired outcome. Comprehending how to raise our energy while breaking down old patterns that drain our energy, allowing us to align more fully with source energy, is integral.

Respectfully, all energy is sentient. All stimuli are energy. All stimuli are sentient energy, conscious of a systemic process that can bring us up or drag us down. The mind uses energy to process and break down scenarios, looping the conclusions back into the mind. Purifying our energy using appropriate stimuli supports a heightened source energy level. Erratic thought patterns, such as worry, fear, or negativity, distort our connection to purified source energy, leading to incoherence.

The conscious mind tends to think while the subconscious mind drives. Learning to pause, to slow down and grow mindful, while asking, "Where did that thought, or response come from?" This in turn slows down our response mechanisms, allowing a more mindful approach to life's challenges and a more conscious respect for the situation.

Currently people tend to become conscious in reflection only when they are in trouble or they're experiencing a highly negative response to their actions. Experiencing inexplicable conflicts nudges us to grow more aware of our destructive behaviors. This usually happens when neurotic thought patterns bump up against conscious attitudes, resulting in a contrary role in our life we need to face.

Conflict is often based on instinctual attitudes clashing with our conscious selves. It is from this well of unconsciousness that the conscious mind matures and develops. Jung states that the unconscious mind is the source of our human consciousness. The unconscious is the actual original mind of humankind. Comprehending our unconscious attitudes and behaviors will enhance humanity's consciousness.

Sharing a Smile

I didn't realize it at the time. While riding my bicycle to the penny candy store, I came across a man wearing leather-strapped sandals. Most people wore flip-flops by the beach, so his shoes caught my attention. He was exiting the store that once supplied a week's worth of candy for a nickel. Stunned that the shop had converted to a bookstore, he noticed my disappointment and started a conversation. I remember commenting on his shoes.

A few weeks later, I came home from riding my bicycle and this same man with the leather sandals was sitting on the patio with my mother, having a conversation. I recognized him from his shoes. He visited often that summer. I would later learn this man wearing the leather shoes was Ram Das, or Richard as we knew him.

I rediscovered Richard as an adult. His teachings continue to touch my heart and soul. His takeaway on the ego verses soul resonates as truth. Ego is the part of us that dies with the physical body. It expresses bodily sensations from a vantage point of me/mine; I want, I see, and I hear. It is a software program for the hard drive experience of self. Ego connects with Ego.

Soul is the level of being that does not die. It is the eternal personality individualized as the witness to ego. It is our conscious identity. While in a soul state or conscious state, we can connect with others on this level. It is impossible to connect on a soul level while coming from ego. Souls connect with souls.

Spirit is the level of divinity, the spark of life within every living entity. It is the level we access through the universal field. A glimpse of something greater that permeates the field for brief moments in time. It is accessible only from a conscious soul level. Spirit connects with Spirit.

Consciously connecting to the soul of another, we recognize our connection is the eternal spirit of the divine. Graced by a level of soul expression, we can see the whole picture of humanity's potential. We see the body as a vehicle for divine expressions. This level continues after the body loses breath. When we see ourselves as souls, we see everyone as souls.

Meditating on actualizing our human blueprint is a great place to start connecting deeply with humanity's conscious awakening. Delving deeper within ourselves to serve the greater good of our global community supports each being in the microcosm of the universal process of life.

Quantum physics is the most truthful and accurate science available on the planet in comprehending the aspects of human connection to the universe. The first premise of consciousness is creating our life experience. While the pictures of our mind are broadcast into the world and our consciousness shapes the reality we experience in life.

Energy to the Second

Consciousness plays a vital role in shaping life experiences. There is also the collective consciousness that shapes the collective reality. We each have our own personal consciousness that affects how we see the world. Our personal perspectives coincide with how the world appears, as a whole.

Physics connects to biology as the brain transmits images in our mind, manifesting the idea into reality. This is how we "know" something will happen or hold expectations of specific outcomes to specific behaviors. The chance we are manifesting is stymied in the unconscious.

The process takes chemistry from the brain and transmits it throughout the body via the bloodstream. Blood provides nutrition as well as information to the cells, tissues, and organs of the body. The more positive the images in the mind, the more beneficial the chemistry to sustain life is released into the bloodstream.

Conversely, the more negative or detrimental our thoughts are, the more detrimental the chemistry is for the body.

The chemistry of the brain is a complement to the picture in the mind. The chemistry of the brain regulates chemistry in the blood responsible for cellular information that supports normal genetic expression or not. Because the picture in the mind, the thought response, is responsible for cellular behavior, we begin to understand how consciousness is the underlying factor responsible for how we feel and how character is shaped through life.

The more conscious we become, the more control we have over our life's direction. Listening to mass appeal, our highest self often leads us down a road that may initially feel good yet eventually leaves us feeling alone and unfulfilled. Tapping into our higher mind, we send patterns into the field of what we truly want.

Discerning the conscious mind from the unconscious can be tricky. Ego is our higher self driving our life experiences. The ego can offer a higher attunement of soul expressions with more joy and happiness. The ego can alert us to dangers via intuition and guide us away from harm as a protector of sorts. That's when the ego is operating via the conscious mind.

The conscious mind rarely correlates to ego. Ego is mainly the autopilot process of the subconscious mind we programmed as a kid. Ego is mainly based on fear. The old traumas and sabotaging patterns of our deepest insecurities are found in the ego.

Self-Mastery

Mastering our higher self requires moving from our subconscious ego patterns of addictive programs and behaviors skewing our soul's expression. This healing supports our light emerging. Since ego can distort our perspective on life, healing it is like shattering a lens of our traumas.

Breaking free from the pains that distort our soul and ego from being in the here and now. Merging our inner world is a lifestyle choice that can take a lifetime to master. It's a continuous heightened awareness of how we feel and what we choose to focus on.

Balancing our need for soul expression and ego expression, we learn to weigh our actions with the results. Physical bodily sensations balanced with our wants and desires come into question. What are our basic needs? We all require air, water, and nutrients to survive. Comfort and warmth are essential as well.

We need to eliminate as well as intake. And as humans, we need love. Nurturance is an essential part of being. Intimate relationships where we are respectfully touched as well as self-love offer a deeper connection to life and to supreme love. Aside from these basic needs, all else is considered a want or a desire.

Learning the language of wanting and needing shifts the body into receiving all that we need effortlessly while paving a path to acquire all that we desire. Changing our language changes the energy drains we place in the field. By stating, "I want," rather than "I need," something shifts the energy pattern emitted and received. It creates a more precise communication for a more precise outcome to be had. It clarifies our light.

Discerning where our decisions come from by reevaluating our needs and wants shifts the subconscious patterns of addiction. It breaks down the old self so we may create a new self-aware being able to run on heightened, healthy, subconscious levels. Taking time to slow down prior to taking actions, fully knowing our actions ripple back to us from the field, puts us in charge of the life we are living. We are no longer victims of our circumstances; we are the cocreators of our life's dreams come true.

Through awareness of which actions are taken that lead us to despair, we can reverse engineer the steps used to manifest the desireless outcome. Recalling that thoughts precede actions, we are more capable of seeing the thought patterns used to generate the undesirable states we find ourselves in. This takes time. Journaling can help put it into perspective. I know I learn faster when I write things out. Seeing it makes it easier to comprehend.

Energy to the Third

All thoughts and actions go through the universal field, the universal mind, the one source. This universal consciousness holds the frequency of our every thought. We understand that thoughts alter our internal environment; they also affect our external realm. Controlling thoughts, pausing before acting is important since all thoughts emit a frequency into the field, grounding them into reality. Thoughts acted upon, and unacted upon, go into the unified field regardless of actions taken.

The present moment is where we connect. The present connects us into the field. The field is the sole governing agency of particles. Einstein knew the field controls particles. He stated it repeatedly in his writings. This self-governing agency of particles is replicated throughout living matter, including the human body.

DNA offers a similar self-charging scalar energy system sequenced in patterns replicating the bioelectrical and biophysical matrix of the living world. Healing energies are prevalent in creating new protected habitats for humanity to explore humanely sentient experiences.

When we access the field, we go beyond the body. We go beyond the mind. Going beyond mind and body changes the body and the mind. To truly heal imbalances from starting up again, we must practice. Repetition is the only way these changes cascade into long-term changes in our personality. Einstein mentioned, "There's no place in new physics for field and matter. The field is the only reality. All else is a projection from the mind."

Obtaining a heightened frequency, with information beyond normal sensory perception, offers insights greater than ordinary reality. It takes practice. The lower frequency of our current reality inhabits the body in space and time. It separates us from everything else. It keeps us searching outside ourselves for love, care, and health.

Our senses support these variances as part of the material world we choose to live in. While the field takes a familiar environment of people, places, or things and reviews how disconnected from heightened emotions we are when we're linked to the familiar environment. It offers a perspective of what is and what can be.

People are comparable to bioelectromagnetic grounding rods. When a charge or frequency is expelled from thoughts, someone in the field will receive it. This is how we impact each other in unconscious ways. The more emotion attached to the thought, the more charge it builds in the collective consciousness of the field. The energy of groups can be exceptionally powerful for good or not-so-good outcomes for humanity.

Tools we can use to ground anger, sadness, or fear are punching pillows or getting out in nature and focusing on beauty. Running, biking, hiking, or swimming. Essentially moving the body to recharge and dispel negative thoughts and energy stored up is good for the planet, let alone for us.

Writing it out then burning the emotional energy with a clear intention is another way to release and transmute unwanted energy we hold. We can use neurolinguistic programming to visualize and recalibrate the scenario since the mind is unable to distinguish between physicalness in the here and now and thoughts in the mind.

More steps can be taken to find the source of negative or addictive energy patterns. Entering meditation with a clear, concise goal to discover if the energy is embedded in the ego or within the soul. If emotion is from the present or the past. This is one way to identify where deeper healing needs to take place. Modern energy psychology is available if we need someone to guide us through deeper traumas.

Always remember to center into a higher conscious state prior to asking for guidance. It's crucial to ask from a higher state of grace than from a wounded place. The ego can be tricky and give us false insights when our intentions are not rooted in our highest heart-based self. As we make these tweaks in ourselves, notice how the world reflects our conscious choices.

When we come from our highest self and greet others from this place of distinction, we hold space for them to join us. We allow them to reap the benefits of our choices so they too may grow more aware in their discovery of their authentic selves.

Changing ourselves is pivotal in changing our family, our community, and our global civilization. Taking a conscious stance from me to we is how we achieve a unified planetary group of heightened beings known as the human race.

SECTION 3

A World Made in Our Image

CHAPTER 10

A New Day Dawning

The world is full of self-help gurus who want to guide us into our greatest life experiences. They offer foolproof systems that work for most people, yet there's no magic one-size-fits-all that suits everyone getting rid of the old and ushering in the new. Not everyone gets their sought-after results, no matter how much money they spend. That's because we are the only ones who can change our habits to become a new person with a new body having new experiences. There's only one tool to propel us into the life of our dreams, and that's consciousness.

Consciousness is the awareness of our actions and reactions to life. The willingness to accept our responsibility in how we are creating the life we are living and the gumption to do something differently. Understanding how the human brain biologically works offers insights in how we can consciously choose to do things differently.

The following is a basic how-to for those of us seeking to align with heightened results. Once centered, take a moment to think about it. Then consider taking a moment to truly listen. The response offered will always feel appropriate. It will always be the true essence of our heart. The response offered may not be what we think we want. It seems to follow an innate path of higher sourced guidance. A softened version of self that no longer needs to compete for attention. We are the ones we've been seeking. We become the I Am.

I Am willing to develop an entirely new relationship with my true self. I Am courageous and capable of fully embracing, no matter how difficult it may seem at times, an updated version of thinking, acting, and being, humbled and graciously allowing the old, outdated ways to fade away to new, upgraded possibilities aligned in proper human actions present. Saying "Yes!" to a higher level of guiding wisdom measured and cohered in 0.1 hertz mitigates a global unification on the planet that's never been measured before. Who's with me in embracing what can be? It's time!

No matter how difficult life appears, there is always room for change. We may not know how or what to change, but guaranteed, it's happening. We understand the energetic fingerprint exists in the field, meaning if someone has done it before, the energy signature is readily available to replicate the result. Having a clear plan gets us there once we take decisive action. Succeeding in the plan requires discipline and of course the courage to see it through.

Clarity of connecting through the unified field. Regenerating the planet's resources, activating energy from source and purified water from quantum devices able to pull purified water out of the air, especially in coastal areas. Think of the abundance for all beings once we adopt a cooperative mentality. *"A Beautiful Mind"* was written describing just the nature of cooperation in quantum mechanics and the economic model widely used.

Clarity of what I truly want and desire to see individually and collectively. Write it. State it. Embrace it as if it already exists. Get excited about who you are becoming. The person you are proudly connecting with in your own human form. The alliances and support you share with those in your family, community, region, and states.

The mindsets that lock us into our relationships infused from birth expressing as young adults, twentysomethings, and so forth play out as patterns we continuously repeat. Who are we becoming? No worries about who we are leaving behind.

Who are we becoming? Shout it! Write it down! Own it! Imagine it in full detail. Get clear on what we want rather than what we no longer want. Clear intentions vibrate to universal source energy and are reflected to us as reality.

The Art of Living

There is an art to creative living. The rational mind will argue with the artistic mind. The conscious and unconscious minds act like a ping-pong match at times when we are not in heart-based coherence. Our energy essence is the natural creator, the magician, and the driver of our experiences in life.

Wanting a better life, health, job, travel opportunities, lover, or spouse. Wanting to feel happier in relationship with … Wanting to experience more joy daily. Whatever it is that suits your fancy, claim it as if it already was yours. Move from "I want" to "I have." I have an amazing new life. I have an amazing new lover. I have more than enough money to live well.

Setting intention to instruct our energy systems through the field is fundamental in receiving the desired result. Ground down firsthand. Access the sweet spot within the field using breath prior to intentionally writing, affirming, and saying precisely what we want to experience. Once aligned, keep breathing in heart-based coherence, getting clear and as detailed as possible. This is stage one to mastering the life of our dreams.

Remember our inner reality is the basis of all outer experiences and events leading to the experiences we have. Drawing from our inner realm offers everything necessary to generate the outer experience. Tuning an idea into material form as an experience should flow easily and naturally when connected to source. This fluidity is indicative of our alignment.

When we find obstacles and blocks moving forward, there may be a reason for the resistance. Possibly an empirical guiding force nudging us in a different direction. Accepting that we are a fraction of source energy, possessing highly creative powers supports a shift in time. It involves relating to nature's rhythms of day and night, seasons, and tides.

Releasing manmade time restrictions sets the stage for pure creation to be unleashed. Pure creation cannot be bound by manmade time frames since time isn't linear, happenings take place simultaneously, interdimensionally within universal time spans. Linear time equates to each, and every moment attuned to producing rather than being. Being here and now, experiencing the present.

Most failures happen when cultural time presses in on our creative time space. We ran out of time. What if time really was outdated and no longer present in the new times? The now? This refers to a more intuitive way to live. A way in which we naturally approach life with instinctive actions and methods that are in truth timeless.

The magical ease in which work can happen outside space and time. The process of life unfolding to secure all our basic needs outlined by Maslow's hierarchy are no longer a worry. Our basic needs are continuously supplied for a more fulfilling life experience to happen.

To shift the interval atmosphere from the current global model to this natural experiential awareness is key to unifying longevity and happiness. While initiating anew may result in chaotic occurrences as our old bumps into our new. The old often no longer feel comfortable and may feel uncomfortable. Depending on our awareness, it may or may not be expressed negatively to those around us.

Navigating through the discomfort is made easier using deep breaths. This offers a moment to pause and reset our awareness of the goal at hand rather than the response to the sensations moving through us. Creative awareness doesn't appreciate confined restraints on its expression. It knows what supports its expansion and what shrinks its heightened awareness.

Our choices of life-affirming expression sometimes mean letting go and saying goodbye to outdated friends and ways of acting. It means we actively release who and what no longer serves our higher purpose. We consciously choose exalted awareness and lightness of being. We accept our lightness and our inevitable process at this initiating stage of human growth in coherence.

The creative cohered being has full access to the living library's records of all past experiences lived and imagined. The living library of all life's experiences are coded within the DNA of every person/being. Living naturally cohered allows us instant access to the vast knowledge eternally available since events have electromagnetic signatures. Reading these electronics becomes innate knowledge.

A Quantum Life

The concept that we are fractals of one living being entrained in the quantum world of energy for eternity is difficult for many to grasp. This entanglement, if you will, defines the unity of each being within the whole of life. Living this truth supports humanity shifting into a cocreative sustainable global community of humankind: conscientious, benevolent, and cooperative. The precept that life is connected through energy is woven delicately through proven scientific methods aligned in spiritual traditions of the world currently entrenched within imbalances in society. Balancing inner spiritual wisdom with outer scientific knowledge we refine this delicate weave of innate wisdom transcended.

Science and religion have been the cause of argument for eons, setting the stage for a competitive rather than cooperation prognosis. Quantum physics addresses the need to compete by showing how nature is cooperative in essence and how we are entangled in the cooperative mode of conduct, whether we are conscious of this fact or not. The most valid principles of quantum physics are the primal mechanisms of how the universe operates.

Quantum physics offers a worldview completely different from the world we've chosen to believe in. Quantum physics exposes an underlying consciousness continuously engaged in consumer-driven competitive notions separating humankind from our innate power. The innate power to make our dreams come true, a personal utopia, or for others, a heaven on Earth experience.

The world we live in, the world we see, is created unconsciously by the mental programs people are running through their unconscious minds, based on misinformation passed down from generation to generation. The misinformation we've accepted as truths includes genetics, social norms as well as how humans developed into modern day humans.

Knowledge is power, and a lack of it is a lack of power. Humans have been energetically disempowered through the course of history, resulting in victimhood mentality that's hit epidemic proportions. It's time for an empowered cohered collective known as humanity to populate the globe.

Are you ready to accept the truth of where we come from and how powerful we truly are as cocreators in life? Accepting new knowledge can enhance personal power and, when directed cooperatively, has the power to create a harmonious global community akin to everyone living a happy, healthy life.

Think about it! We all want to prosper, to be seen and heard, to have the freedom to express our creative selves, and to be respected for our unique perspective. We want to engage in community and feel we belong and are useful in supporting the whole. We want to feel loved. This doesn't have to be a dream.

It's already happening in villages and towns around the world. People are coming back to the simplicity of respecting each other for what they bring to the table, recognizing we are all human and imperfect. Yet we are all cooperatively working toward supporting one another on a path to living more divinely.

The Body New

Falsehoods we now know to be true litter history. We once thought the world to be flat, yet today, we recognize the flat concept is not accurate. The same is true of humans coming from chimpanzees. Chromosome 2 clearly defines a genetic fusion that took place, enhancing neural capacity for compassion to present within the human heart.

Believing our genes control our cells and our life is another nontruth. Genes have nothing to do with cell membranes communicating how to replicate. Cell membranes are information processors analyzing incoming signals and adapting the performance mechanism within cell systems. This mechanism complements the environment, proving we can change our cells functions to support health and longevity.

Cell membranes adjust their biology by adjusting their liquid crystal semiconductors. A computer's semiconductor mimics the body since computers are made in the image of human biology. These microprocessors have gates and channels that operate precisely the same way our bodies do. Silicon computer chips match the structure of a cell membrane and information processor.

A cell's surface antennae are hair like processors inherent to an individual's higher self. The identity of a cell is found in the field of the cell. The "self" is a broadcast being received by the antennae of our cells correlating to our experiences and in turn how we feel.

The cell's electrical activity responds via the field and is apparent in transplant patients who receive an organ from a donor and exhibit characteristics of a different personality shortly after the transplant. Transplant patients often adopt traits from the host via the field.

This instills the reception of two personalities blended into the one, proving life exists outside the body. We incarnate when an embryo appears with the identical self-antennae in our innate energy field. This self is broadcast into matter, into being, and into life in that body.

The Collective Broadcast System

Every living being receives a broadcast from something greater than our collective. The body can be compared to a TV set as Dr. Bruce Lipton likes to say. Concluding that a broadcast signal can be received by anybody housing our specific antennae, regardless of race, gender, religious or economic status. It's all energy.

The collective broadcast system via the field can be thought of as an individual "eye" or a collective vision. When we come together, we move from the outdated theory of evolution to a community of collective consciousness. Humanity is no longer a victim of its circumstances; we become a heightened super organism able to work, organize, and prosper as one.

We move away from groups of people fighting each other, kind of like how an autoimmune disease fights its host body. Humanity is reacting to the times in a similar fashion as a group of cells attacking themselves. Humanity's self-destruction obsession is out of balance and in need of repair.

Only when we realize we are all part of the same source energy, one living entity, will we experience our full potential. Only then will modern diseases fail to threaten humankind, and only then will peace on Earth reign as healthy people take the lead in creating their dreams come true as a collective conscious race.

The world is in transition. The current transition is one into wholeness and community. It begins with individuals cleaning up our thoughts and habitual patterns. This influences families to restructure and communities to rebuild. We're at a critical time in history to do it differently. This is where we have power to create. What are we creating? What beliefs are we holding onto as true?

We comprehend the mind of a child is the absorbent mind. What we teach our children in the first seven years of life is imprinted in the mind of each child and replayed throughout adulthood. Quantum physics shows the current reality we're experiencing is an illusion. In truth, we live in a quantum universe.

One Heart, One Mind

When we look at the mind, we recognize there are two minds: the conscious mind and the unconscious. The conscious mind is the creative mind. This is the mind that makes us different from others. It is the mind that develops our personality and shapes our character. The subconscious mind is the habitual mind. It learns and experiences repeatedly, forming patterns and automatic responses. It houses learned behaviors like walking that rarely need to be relearned. The conscious mind boasts our wishes and our creative desires. The subconscious houses our programs from childhood.

These minds work similarly to a tablet or phone respectively. The conscious mind is the actual hard-wired device, and the subconscious is the programs we load onto the device. When we get a new device, it only runs the programs we download onto it.

Kids operate the same way. The first seven years are the formulative years, the time when we download behaviors by observing how others behave. Kids don't have anything to be conscious of; they are in an imaginative mode of make-believe. Playing with trucks or dolls seems very real to them as the brain is subconsciously recording all the experiences happening around them.

Their environment is shaping their responses to their life. It is observing and downloading how to behave via a theta brain wave activity used in hypnosis. When we think about it, we learn how to behave by downloading others' behaviors. As we grow and mature, we act out these behaviors as our normal social standard and become a replication of those around us in our formulative years. We become a fractal of their being, replicating generations of their dysfunction.

How different would you be if your parents and mentors in early childhood understood your brain was developing from experiences in theta brain activity. The hypnotic state of the subconscious responsible for recording our day-to-day nuances subconsciously during our first seven years of life.

Psychologists agree that 70 percent of the program's children pick up in early childhood are disempowering beliefs. Beliefs that we aren't good enough or we can't do that. Most of the day, adults operate from these unconscious programs. This means that adults barely use their conscious mind.

Basic thinking turns our conscious mind over to the subconscious. We do this for walking, driving, talking, and acting. There are times when acting unconsciously is equated with self-sabotaging behaviors. These behaviors can slip in from deep, unresolved issues of self-worth, etc. Unless we were fortunate to have empowered parents who instilled empowering beliefs within us during our formulative years, it's not uncommon to have issues in need of review.

CHAPTER 11

Reflecting Sets Our Compass on Course

If you're like me and experienced a disempowering upbringing, then have no fear! There's a way to break out of the self-defeating cycles we learned along the way. We don't have to be the product of a carbon-copied parent or guardian. We can be our true, authentic self with self-empowering beliefs and actions that support our life's highest potential and that of the children stepping onto the planet.

Believing we can eliminate the victim mentality allows us to step into a creative conscious reality. Staying mindful every step of the way allows us to recognize when we fall out of consciousness. This awareness allows us to change our behaviors and to become heightened in our awareness of how our words, actions, and feelings respectively result in our experiences.

What we experience can change into what we want to experience as we inherently begin to make subtle changes drawing life to us rather than letting our subconscious replay outdated experiences of the programs that no longer serve our greater fulfillment. Removing self-sabotaging beliefs may take time, courage, and consistency. It also takes the willingness to face our reality and see how our actions truly deem our experiences.

Every human has a choice to choose the programs we operate from. When we all choose to enhance our innate nature, we choose to embody a consciousness that unifies the global consciousness of humanity. Now humans are no longer a single individualized unit; we are a superhuman, an innately conscious entity symbiotically supporting all life. Wow! Imagine how it would feel if the entire world fell in love at the same time!

When we fall in love, the subconscious mind gets overridden with the conscious experience of being in love. We disconnect from embedded programs and operate in the creative conscious level of hopes, wishes and desires. This lasts until we allow the mind to start thinking. This moves us from the creative brain into the dichotomy brain, the dual action of a ping-pong match.

Remember the brain has left and right hemispheres that oscillate between rationalizing and creating. Our subconscious mind sabotages the elated feelings of bliss by forcing the old programs to run while the mind is caught up in a mental ping-pong match oscillating between this or that. Remaining in a state of love or deep gratitude keeps the mind consciously creating the feelings of bliss or dreams come true. Only when we stop the unconscious programs of mental masturbation do we experience true happiness.

What will it take to make the move from mindless acts to consciously creating a life worthy of our highest goals? An expanded bounty of pure creation for the good of all on the planet? It's time for parents to heal their hurts and teach their children a different option for life on the planet. A higher level of awareness of what can be and what already exists for many.

This is true because, thankfully, more and more parents are choosing conscious parenting. This mindful approach empowers children to retain their innate connection to source energy while embracing their fullest potential more readily.

Since young people adapt the beliefs and illnesses of those they live with, conscious parenting ensures they develop humanely, despite their genetic heredity. The environment and lifestyle support coherence to naturally express. Imagine a world where the environment and lifestyle people chose enhanced life expectancy and supported fulfillment and creative expression while allowing all beings to thrive and be the best version of themselves. This is possible when parents choose to practice conscious parenting.

Julia Bella

My mother, Julia, was considered mentally ill, yet her tactics for remaining compassionate and kind were unmatched. She often cooked for neighbors who were ill or unable to nourish themselves. She believed food was our greatest gift to share as it nourished not only the body but also brought conversation that nourished the heart and soul of everyone.

When we were ill, she made food to heal us. She poured her heart into every meal she made. When food didn't help us feel better, she made tea. She was aware of the properties of nourishment on a level that nudged me along my path in life. When tea failed, she found homeopathy. A medical doctor was the last resort. This is how we were raised.

After my sister became ill with a most tragic stroke while attempting suicide, I became adamant I would spend the rest of my life helping people feel better. I was twelve when I found her blue-faced. Thank goodness I had the gumption to pound her chest with both fists, forcing air back into her lungs. She's become a living angel in my life, continuously teaching me how to be a better human being.

Always kind mannered, she emulates a high being effortlessly. In retrospect, I've never heard her say an unkind word about another or swear or raise her voice. I sometimes wonder how we came from the same parents. Her gentle nature is a rare gift I feel blessed to have bestowed upon me.

Sharing gifts of compassion from the heart is what my mother instilled in my sister at an early age. Her mindful mannerisms programmed into her child empowered my sister to overcome her stroke. This in turn allowed her to create her wishes and desires into reality. Unlimited potential allowed them to create a conscious world to thrive in. Most children will choose a gentle world with a balanced environment to thrive in. Therefore, conscious parenting is imperative.

It's never too late to rebirth, to outgrow our programs from early childhood. Comprehending how subconscious programs create the life we are living helps the rational mind grasp our current programs so we can discern where and how to do things differently, changing our experiences.

Reprogramming the Old

The conscious mind consistently recognizes we can learn and adapt to manifest our desires and dreams. Yet subconscious behaviors fail to realize the habits formed, resulting in longer periods to disengage from and reprogram new habits. This is usually prevalent as repeated patterns until we make a choice that transcends the scenario offering a new outcome. A great depiction of this is the classic movie *Groundhog Day.*

Using hypnosis or theta brain wave activity is where we can override the subconscious mind. It's the sweet spot where our subconscious receives new habits and new beliefs. What we experience during this theta state processes in the subconscious. Theta naturally occurs at the start and close of each day. As we rise and fall from sleep, it's the place in the mind we are highly suggestive to reconditioning. Neurolinguistics or guided meditations as well as meditations have great results when utilized during theta brain states.

Another area we can shift the subconscious mindset is through habitual repetition. Doing something repeatedly breaks the cycle of the habit mind. The adage "Fake it until we make it" comes in handy here. When we believe we are healthy, our body responds in kind by making the chemistry of health. Repeating the intention until we actualize the effect long term. Repetition reprograms the subconscious into a healthy habit, running automatically.

Mindfulness

Mindful meditation heightens our awareness of our senses. This form of medication, enacted with a laser focus on what we are feeling in the moment, hones our internal compass. By observing our sensations without judgment, we gain control over our body, allowing breath to guide us deeper into states of nothingness.

Becoming nothing where no sensation deters our focus is the goal of mindful meditation.

Having mastered mindfulness, we become witnesses to life's experiences, no longer drawn into personal dramas. We can view life from a vantage point of peaceful understanding as an observer without judgment. This instills a peaceful energy that ripples outwardly, affecting the field as well as our immediate environment. We can shift situations around us simply by being present, being mindful.

Most people blindly accept worldviews without questioning the origin or source behind them. Most worldviews are propagated by special interests targeting the subconscious mind to consume the insights as a fact for personal gain. These myth perceptions are flawed views disempowering humanity and the Earth at an alarming rate.

As a wellness instructor for over forty years, I can attest to the fact that our current model of health care is in disrepair. Health-care workers are overburdened with the number of ill patients. We do not have the ability to manage the growing number of ill people. It's our personal responsibility to take our health back into our own hands. Accepting we are our own best healers able to restore normal cell functions.

Life as we know it isn't sustainable. Continuously relying on internet shopping to deliver goods to our front door is unsustainable. Allowing our children to spend hours in front of a blue screen is unsustainable for their long-term energy. Teaching competition over cooperation is unsustainable. What will it take for humanity to wake up and do things differently?

It seems the pandemic era of global lockdown enhanced a

sleeper mode ensuring people bought more online and played more violent video games. The ease of not leaving home increased instant gratification connections in the brain. Purchasing items not needed became a comfort most refuse to let go of. Gamers are facing the addiction to adrenaline-pumping reactions of nonstop killing, rewiring neural networks informing the mind and body the need for this behavior to feel alive. Aggression is a shadow side of human nature.

The new norm that emerged postpandemic is one of awkward social distance whereby people are uncomfortable having a conversation face-to-face. How does it end? Where does this norm meet a new? It's time to wake up to the fact of how dim humanity has grown and how to rekindle the human heart at 0.1 hertz.

One Heart, One Planet

History is on track to repeat itself. Technology is making huge leaps and bounds, potentially taking humanity into an arena disconnected from source, the creative spark of life. The essence of all living things, beings, plants, animals, minerals, and elements in the universe carry a spark of life. This life comes from somewhere. That somewhere is source, and source is being dimmed in light of the gadgets that distract our attention.

Teachings from thousands of years back litter the world with clues of source energy. Scientists and physicists have isolated the spark of life in numerous experiments over the past hundred or so years. Religious leaders have molded their words attempting to emulate the power of source from an ego standpoint for centuries.

Yet very little is taught to our young about the essence of source energy or the governing power of the universe.

The outdated story of who we are as human beings and how our world operates is changing. It's time. A shift in thinking is happening and has reached proportions that are unstoppable. The choice now falls on everyone. Will we choose cooperation as a human race upon Earth or choose to continue competing for life with all other life-forms on the planet? Tick tock, people. Tick tock.

Seeing Heart to Heart

The power of choice is based on values. What we believe instills values in us at an early age. By age seven, our values and beliefs are hard wired into our entire body system, through every cell and neural connection. Our biochemistry is set up to support our choices by these values and beliefs we picked up during the first years of our life.

We come into the world as a spark of light. A spark from source anchored into flesh and blood. Carrying a blueprint of who we are and what we are to accomplish in life. From the moment our spark is instilled, we begin feeling the world around us. As our heart and brain develop in the second trimester of gestation, we begin processing our environment. The internal regulating system as well as our external atmosphere.

Our host, or mother, is a filter for what we will feel as her chemistry is directly linked to our experience. Once born into the world, our heightened state of awareness, which was amplified by the fluid surrounding us in the womb, softens. The external environment takes on a new phase. A phase of learning through the five senses of sight, touch, audio, sensation, and taste.

As a new being in a formulated realm of existence, we spend the next few years attempting to communicate while in a hypnotic state of theta brain waves. This state is the frequency of subconscious programming. By age seven, we are programed with the beliefs and responses we will use to navigate through life. These programs will run subconsciously without our conscious awareness until we have a need to review them.

At some point, most people will have a crisis that requires them to change course. A life-shifting event of proportions that leads them to review how they approach life and how they may make changes to live more authentically.

Energy is everywhere, even in the human body. Our cells are specialized in conducting electrical currents. Electricity is required for the nervous system to send signals throughout the body and to the brain, making it possible for us to move, think and feel. Emotions are energetic imprints playing an integral part of how we feel and how our body regenerates.

Today is the beginning of the rest of your life. What life will you create? What experiences will you have that propel you into forward discovery and happiness? What choices will you make to ensure your health and happiness are extended long term for life? Yes, choices we make today will impact how we feel tomorrow. Literally the choices we make impact our physiological systems as well as our future outcomes.

CHAPTER 12

A New Paradigm Emerging

It's long been noted that we live in an energy world. Quantum physics proves every thought and every emotion we experience is entangled in what is known as the quantum field. The field holds possibilities. Possibilities of multiple outcomes dependent on the energy associated with the experience. Energy is a catalyst for manifesting our thoughts into reality. And reality is a direct reflection of how we feel. Sound like a sci-fi film? Well, you're not too far from the truth.

The twenty-first century launched a plethora of movies supporting magical mystery powers. Movie franchises like Harry Potter or Marvel's Avengers, as well as the myriad of Netflix series like *The Magicians* and *The 4400*. There is a reason why movie themes are alluding to the fact that people are magical beings. We are. Human potential has been dumbed down for centuries to retain a level of consumerism over self-awareness.

What if everyone had the power to create beauty and harmony just by thinking about it? The ability to generate the life of their dreams without having to buy anything on the internet. The ability to communicate through aether without having to pick up a phone. That's the future of humanity. When we can give up the need to consume at the level we've grown accustomed to, we can achieve the unimaginable.

The world is a magical realm of possibilities and we, the magicians, have allowed humankind to tell us that we are ordinary beings only good for working eight hours a day to spend more than we earn to live a life that's worth living, wearing the right clothes, driving the right car, and believing that this is the good life. This belief is being challenged, and the findings are remarkable. Not only is the reality of consumerism breaking down, but the rise of incredibly talented young people is also leaving their mark on the world.

The Next Generation Gets It

One of of the youngest and best-known activists of our time, Greta Thunberg's passionate awareness on the importance of climate change made her a world leader nearly overnight. Her heartfelt compassion to cohere a sustainable global community touched the hearts and souls of many around the world, catalyzing others to follow in her footsteps.

Today's young people want a different world from the one they're inheriting. These highly attuned beings are aware of the intricacies of their high selves. They fully grasp human potential and are unwilling to settle for anything else. They are patiently awaiting humanity's rise in cohesion so they may be fully seen and heard.

So how do we move humanity from a mundane dissociated life into an interactive extraordinary life? It's simple. We challenge everything we think we know. We seek deeper understanding based on heart coherence, truth. We infuse new knowledge of how this world operates and how we as human beings can excel in the new paradigm. Are we ready for that?

We've all been taught similarly from birth how to respond to life's experiences. We have been conditioned to react to our experiences by mimicking those around us. Our theta brain state absorbed and reinforced the responses of those around us. We learned how to live their life, not ours.

This hypnotic state conditioned our mind, infusing neural connections that mimicked our parents, siblings, or whomever we spend time with. Their personality is meshed in our personality. It's where we learned to subconsciously become them. And where we need to dig deep into so we may eliminate the conditions that molded us into consumers rather than creators.

I first learned how powerful thoughts are as a kid swinging on a swing with my sister. We would imagine new and different flavors of gum or Barbie dolls. We were always surprised when these flavors showed up the next week or Barbie all a sudden got a teen friend, Skipper.

I didn't understand back then, but now it's apparent. Thoughts flow in and out of the field. It's our actions on these thoughts that manifest a reality. While we didn't make the watermelon bubble gum, our heartfelt thoughts of it helped bring it to fruition.

Balance

Inhumanity ebbs and flows but never really goes away. You would think that by this day and age, humans would understand that war is a tactic of the unevolved unconscious part of our collective; humanity operating from an ego-based fear.

We as a human race are capable of much greater feats. Cooperating, we can find ways through our differences. We can cocreate a loving, lasting realm where we support the unfoldment of everyone's true talents and gifts rather than merely surviving this thing called life.

The universal alignments taking place in space-time resonate in harmony with what I believe humanity is resonating with: 0.1 hertz. This shift in frequency may not last eternally; however, the positive impact it has in unifying human potential within the unified field of source energy is worthy of review. This awareness of what is possible should be considered by every human being on the planet, especially the younger generation who truly want to create a world of their dreams.

The scars we carry from generations of hurts are burdensome to store in the cellular matrix, in the light of our cells, in the information library of our living tissues. This living library houses the entire experiences of humanity. We all have access to this living library of endless information. Only very few take the time to explore the inner realm when there is so much to explore in the outer world.

I often feel like the outer world is a distraction, a distorted place for people to get lost and pretend who they are. A place to put our attention on things, focusing on how we look rather than how we feel. When we feel good, we look good.

When we feel happy, our light intensifies, and our energy field expands around us. People are naturally drawn to our light. Babies recognize us as do animals, and a peaceful harmonious exchange takes place. The energy shared is life affirming, lifting all we meet.

This can also be said of those who are heavy with sadness. Sadness is like a dark cloud dimming our inner light, promoting heavy thoughts that bring us down and perpetuate sadness. We complain and put others down when our inner light is not shining vibrantly. I've often said people may look beautiful but how they feel reveals their true nature. Then again, the outer realm prefers facades over authentic gestures.

What does it mean to live authentically? To open oneself to the inner realm and be guided by the light within? To surrender to the divine nature of one's essence. To be free and caring toward ourselves? To be free and caring toward one another?

This seems to be hastened in today's cultural yoga and meditation craze. I've opened myself to exploring various yoga practices around the world and find the United States is in a frenzy to do yoga as a power workout, barely utilizing breath while rushing through the asanas only to rush back to a fast-paced life, running from one event to another. This is not the root of yoga. Hardly.

The energy we use to stress out or to physically love someone with is the same energy we use to pump up our egos or muscles. This pliable energy field is available on demand to create the life of our dreams. Breathwork is key in accessing our energy potential. Intentionally tapping this energy in the sacral region of the spine via breath and consciously pumping it up our spines into our brains nourishes our mind and body exquisitely.

This innate nourishment is the breath of life. It pushes cerebral spinal fluid into the brain, not only nourishing the brain with nutrients essential for normal functions to take place. It also energetically engages our pineal crystals that act as radio receivers and transmitters connecting us effortlessly to the field.

Daily practice of engaging this level of breath synchronizes our actions into higher levels of abundance. The energy of the brain enhances our overall energy levels, stamina, and abilities to create the life we want.

The analytical, criticizing brain gets less focused while our creative genius brain grows more active connections in daily expressions. This also changes the body's habitual response to moving into the sympathetic nervous system where we are in constant fight-or-flight mode to the parasympathetic nervous system where we are in a relaxed state of grace, able to observe our external life rather than react to it.

Releasing the Old

It's no longer acceptable to know what's out of balance; we need to comprehend how to reintegrate balance into our lives. All the theosophical information we've learned, the science we've learned, offers principles. These fundamental principles allow a heightened awareness to take place. They offer what is possible. Once we learn why we do things, the how becomes easier.

Assigning meaning with practical application makes it easier to integrate it into an experience. We recognize behaviors. We notice if what we are receiving matches our intentions. When our actions line up, our experiences transform. Our learning produces knowledge. This knowledge enriches each experience. Each experience enriches learning. Learning creates greater wisdom, and our heightened awareness results in a heightened emotional state.

When we start feeling emotions, we raise our level of conscious awareness. The more empowered we feel, the more gratitude we hold.

The more whole we feel, the more chemical support we receive from our body. Biochemical feedback teaches our body to understand what the mind intellectually understands. We now embody our truth not only from a standpoint of the mind but from a chemical signature within our body.

This chemistry instructs our genes. Our genes instruct proteins. Proteins are responsible for the structural responses of the body. Proteins are expressions of life. Proteins change our genetic output.

The body gets new information not just from the mind but also from the body. The body is teaching the mind as well by sharing new data and information. Habitual repetition of data input creates subconscious habits. Our body learns how to stay well automatically while we create the life we envision.

These habits run unconsciously within the conscious mind. The mind and body work together to become one. The body knows how to do this innately—second nature so to speak. The body recognizes the mind's habits as familiar and that it is no longer separate from the mind. The body is the mind moving in a mastery of knowledge. Gracefully guided by wisdom.

There are at least ten years of scientific research projects proving that when we separate ourselves from daily routines, when we step out of the familiar, we open ourselves up to having exquisitely divine experiences. We truly become the creators of our life.

One Heart, One Humanity

The greatest tool I've encountered over the years is Heart Math's Heart Coherence Technique. This simple tool has allowed me to teach thousands of clients how to empower their mind and body in the creative force of *now.* To relinquish control over the habitual mind and to open to infinite possibilities within the field.

We understand that the brain changes within two to four days of changing habits. When we bring forward heart coherence, 0.1 hertz, we align the mind in the body. Heart coherence isn't just for yogis. It's been proven to change gene expressions. It allows neuro networks to grow and expand. It expands the proliferation of stem cells. It supports detoxification and regeneration. It supports regulating imbalances within all body systems, and it increases our light emissions from our cells. All this from learning to unplug, sit still, and breathe.

It may even change the way we feel as it rebalances our autonomic nervous system. It calms us and gets us out of fight-or-flight. It brings us into the parasympathetic nervous system. It gently eases tensions from life. Breathe in. It allows us to get a handle on our emotions. Breathe out. It anchors us in the ability to pause before we speak. It supports our cellular respiration and fuels cellular efficiency. Our cells illuminate brightly, and we grow more radiant. We have an increased cellular frequency, and we are more connected to the field. To life. To love.

The field is where we enhance efficacy, luminosity, and regenerative restoring frequencies known in our innately programmed DNA codes. Accessing the field can extend longevity, strengthen immune systems, and even restore normal cell functions. Proteins submit and become resistant to viruses. Viruses die off. Scientific research is showing us more than we can even imagine.

The truth of how powerful we are as light beings. How to heal hurts and regenerate cells. How to live a healthy, happy, long life. It's a simple formula that anyone can master. When we practice this formula, we recognize how valuable practice is. Practice is the healer. It isn't anything outside us. We don't need to ingest it. It's the mere practice of this formula that supports healing to take place.

Committing to practice is when people begin to thrive. We're no longer victims of circumstances. We're cocreating a life filled with extraordinary experiences, limitless energy and stamina, spontaneous healing abilities, longevity, and pure happiness. Imagine one world where we all thrive.

If It Doesn't Feel Good, Don't Do It!

How we think and how we feel has a strong impact on our life. Our physical, emotional life. When we change how we think and feel and go within without distractions, we get beyond what's happening in our body. We get away from our habitual, predictable future. We let go of what is familiar and step into the unknown.

How does it feel? If it feels great, then repeat often. If it feels less than extraordinary, repeat the purification process via mindful heart coherence until it feels better. Kundalini breath work amplifies biophoton expression. Practice ensures we get to live an extraordinary life of our dreams come true.

I've been asked how do you know what it feels like? My response is to equate it to a fond memory, emotional state. Thinking of a beloved, a pet, our grandmother. Grand mamas tend to elate our hearts with the smell of cookies and a warm hug. Animals also warm our excitation for light emissions. When in doubt, expand that warm feeling in the heart and gage how the experience relates. If the feeling doesn't radiate a level of comfort, then leave it behind. No need to revisit that feeling. It can now move to the past.

Part of the creative process is the art of letting go. Allowing the mind and body to disconnect, to release any hold on the past or future. To fully surrender to the now, the present, the unknown takes courage to trust our higher self. To truly accept we are divinely loved and protected.

Learning to surrender to nature requires trust in the divine. Trust that a benevolent being is at the fore of creation, guiding us to be the very best version of ourselves. A higher self if you will. Connecting to the divine means we must access our inner realm, the subconscious mind. Meditation is a gateway to access our divine state of mind when it is infused as a natural lifestyle.

The rational mind barely comprehends how the trillions of cells in the body organize and affirm life. Modern biology, physiology, and psychology have yet to fully comprehend how the divine matrix of the human body functions effortlessly, adapting every second to secure cellular functions occur.

Humans have yet to fully grasp the cooperative nature of nature as represented in form. Surrendering to the mere fact that something larger than who we are is operating our body. Without this knowledge as fact, the following steps into leading a divinely attuned life will fail to manifest the life of one's dreams coming true.

Thoughts house power. They are transmissions of electromagnetic waves/particles that mix with others' thoughts and emotions and form patterns within the electromagnetic field of the community, region, country, and globe. Just as the sky is filled with air molecules, clouds, dust, and such, so too does it contain these mass patterns of electromagnetics.

The overall psychological basis of world events can radically change these patterns. Consider the past year's pandemic. The continuous news programs instilling fear. There is a reason why they are called programs.

Positive constructive thoughts more easily materialize as they are more naturally aligned with divine, life-affirming thoughts and actions in the field. Whereas negative thoughts require much more energy to turn them into reality. Shifting from calm states to being agitated changes our electromagnetics and disrupts our connection to nature. Restoring our connection to calmness as quickly as possible is a process of growing more mindful.

Just Do It!

Getting over negative talk induced from the critical rational mind sometimes takes a little more finesse. Recognizing ways we sabotage our connection to divine life-affirming energy means we must anchor on our path to heightened awareness until our negative self-talk rarely rears itself.

Identifying our choices to consciously create rather than running a subconscious program reduces the risk of replicating the familiar in our daily life. Checking in daily to assess if our results are desired or require fine-tuning is part of the practice and commitment to living a better life. If our outcome is tapping us on our shoulder, saying hello, pay attention. This is not a great result. Then make a conscious choice to change, to do it differently. The choice to start fresh and new.

Healing happens at this level in the field. From a point of intention, we begin creating our extraordinary life. Firstly, a part of our old self must die off. We must release a part of our personality that locks us into past emotional states of physical actions, feelings, thoughts, and habits. Eliminating experiences that no longer serve our highest level of living.

Are our thoughts taking us through life-affirming experiences, supporting our longevity, or are they taking us into habitual nightmarish experiences that are filled with fear, doubt, and worry?

It takes work to manifest the life of our dreams. To secure health and happiness for a long life. It isn't easy. If it were, everyone would be doing it. Yes, everyone would be understanding how to do it. From the yogi teachings, ancient wisdom teachings, metaphysical teachings that I've encountered over the past forty years, the only way to access this level and to sustain it is through practice. To concentrate and to stay fully present. To experience heightened moments in time takes practice. Daily practice. Are you willing to commit to practice?

Mindful meditation shows us how the environment controls us. If we wake up without a vision of our future, then we're accepting our past, repeating it over again each new day. Neurologically speaking, the more we experience or hold attention in a heightened state, the greater our increased neuro environment enhances emotional attachments. We come back to our senses and recognize we must create differently to receive a different result. Otherwise, our personal reality becomes our personality.

Repeatedly talking about hurt or painful experiences that happened years ago locks us into a former version of our self. It deters us from being fully present in the gift of *now*. Thinking, speaking, and feeling show up in our body, reinforcing the same old version of an unhealthy lifestyle, thought process, and body. Our thoughts, words, and actions are energetic things realized in form.

A Simple Technique

Sit up tall with eyes closed and focus on your breath. Claim, "I will be still." Notice what you notice. Focus on your nostrils. Air flowing in and out. Consciously focus. Feel the air curl over the lip on the exhale, Notice the air come down the back of the throat on the inhale.

Allow the breath to fill the lungs, pulling the belly into the naval each breath in while pulling up from the sacral chakra each exhale to fully exhale. Notice how the diaphragm engages, as we move our energy up the spinal column. Feel what you feel as your body gets energized and refueled in light.

Come back to the breath if distracted by mind or sounds or sensations. Come back to the breath. Practice this daily to achieve a victory in redesigning your life.

You may like to visualize the light rising along the spinal column expanding out the heart. You may pull light up from the sacral chakra and down from the 7th chakra to meet in the heart. The light you exhale may appear in a torus formation around your body. You may ask the light to infuse you with healing or knowing or clearing. Remember you are one with the light. Try it.

Practice. Practice catching yourself from thoughts, movements. Train to be victorious. Train to be one with everything and one with no things. Train to tame the animal mind. Train to find liberation in the practice.

Practice is a skill we continuously seek out an edge toward expanding. An edge of greatness that exceeds our previous potential. Our highest potential is just within grasp until the next level occurs.

We keep striving to be a better human being, race and planetary entity.

Begin with five minutes, sit up, and be still. Come back to the breath. Repeat until sitting for thirty, forty, then fifty minutes is achieved. The more we practice, the more energy we generate. Energy is the driving force of all actions.

Remember electrons don't necessarily emit light; what's surrounding them does. Light emissions are responses to electron collisions. A good example is the excitement that happens to molecules in the air when they collide with electrons. The O_2 enhances their level of excitement, emitting a spark or light as they return to normal.

The same is true for humans. When we're excited about something, our internals get activated and speed up. Our heart rate will increase, and we may perspire. Our voice may even go up an octave as we build excitement.

This excitement on an energetic level builds a torus action, a spin of sorts, until the intensity releases and the energy disperse. This results in light emissions on a cellular level. Tantric breath work supports this buildup and release of energy without the need of a partner.

7 Tools to Get There

1. Clarity is the foundation of formulating the life of our dreams. Creating a mission statement of sorts, defining what we want to experience that day, week, month, and year acts as a guide for achieving our goals. I personally like to use a method that asks,

- What're the three top priorities for today, this week, month, year?
- What must be done? What actions must I take to achieve the above?
- What do I want to do? What wants are presenting?
- What're my three personal priorities. What three things will I do for me.?
- What do I need to follow up, to review, and to complete?

These questions, when asked daily, guide us in achieving our goals and can be expanded upon for getting things done on many occasions.

2. Intentions or daily affirmations set the tone for the day. Setting an affirmation, based in heart, tells our body and the field what we would like to experience. Self-talk, we know, is primarily the root of how we think, feel, and believe.

The late Louise Hay used affirmations to reprogram her body from a cancer-filled community of discordant cells into a thriving community of coherent cells. Her remarkable recovery has helped thousands if not millions of people recognize our true power. Louise left us the Hay House platform for learning at hayhouse.com.

I always tell my higher self the kind of day I'd like to have.

3. Journaling offers a means to reflect upon our thoughts, actions, and experiences. Setting a time to journal daily creates a routine, allowing us to create a habit of reviewing who we were and who we are becoming. Journaling helps us refine our clarity.

Morning journaling has worked for me for years; however, I often will take time during the day to reflect through writing. The key is to pause after writing without going back to read what was written. Simply expressing without judgment helps clear the clutter in one's subconscious mind.

Reviewing what's been journaled a week later and highlighting the areas that resonate strongest with where we are at in our experience supports adjusting our thoughts and actions to achieve our goals.

4. Consuming light by incorporating high-energy foods fueled in light begins one meal at a time. When we are shifting from fast foods or convenient foods into foods filled with light, the transition can take time to adapt. I find changing one meal at a time, like lunch, into a light meal, is a great way to begin the process.

Trusting how we feel, noticing the nuances of what seems different in other areas of life supports what works for us and what doesn't necessarily resonate. I've witnessed many who do not feel better simply by changing their diet. Results may not be 100 percent; however, it's a huge step in fueling our body with light for biochemical processes to occur.

A creative perspective of adventure into new flavors and experiences with foods helps. Google offers many recipes for food options that are naturally life enhancing. Vegan recipes are often light-infused food recipes. While eating a variety of colors supports a nutrient-rich internal environment, improving oxygenation essential for cellular respiration.

Meats, fish, and avian food sources are also important for many to feel good. The process of consuming ethically raised foods is coming into question, not only for livestock but all vegetation as well.

The importance of mindful farming, minimal chemical alterations, purified water as well as enriched soil nutrient speak of the soul alignment with our divine matrix in nature. Foods source ethically ensures we live our very best human life. A level never recorded in our lifetime.

5. Mindful movement fuels our battery cells within our mind and body. Mindfulness begins with intention and breath coherence. Walking, Tai Chi, Yoga, and Qigong all support recharging the mind/body balance.

Daily movement should get the blood pumping, ensuring we activate methylation and protein assimilation fueled by endothermic expression of energy release. This thermodynamic notion is prevalent in the expression of normal cell functions. We need energy to regenerate, recover, and feel well. Lack of energy means we are losing voltage, equating to a misconnection of healthy cellular communication leading to unwanted energy blocks within the living matrix known as the body.

This geometrical concept of nuances is proven well in courses available at the Resonance Science Project. These great concepts are available for young adults to fully comprehend the connection of life in the body aligned within universal connections prevalent in daily life occurrences.

6. Quiet time is often overlooked in our current culture. We hustle and bustle to keep up with our social media pages and distracting gadgets. Consciously setting time aside to just be, to sit, and to breathe for twenty minutes a day supports connecting to the field and ensuring we recalibrate our mind/body connection for our highest expression of health and happiness. Quite time means we disconnect from everything & everyone.

For those who have thoughts that distract oneself from sitting still, I highly align with Dr. Joe Dispenza's brilliance. His awareness of how the human mind functions and how to reprogram our true genius successfully helps thousands of people. His site is worth Googling.

7. Sleep is critical for rejuvenating our thought processes as well as our biological systems that keep us actively experiencing life. During sleep, we recalibrate our electrical system, converting light stored in the rods and cones of our eyes for the body to use as fuel. If sleep is an issue, then sleep must be reviewed to accomplish living a long, healthy life. Sleep happens when we convert our feel-good hormones of serotonin to melatonin. This conversion must take place to get to sleep and stay asleep.

If there are issues with sleeping, then reach out to me at whitewillowihealth@gmail.com and I will offer you an assessment of where your body is energy deficient in converting your chemistry for sleep. Resetting chemistry has various roots that we can discuss during our complimentary consult.

CONCLUSION

The greatest gift of being human is the heart of each person. We are a collective, a collective keeper of all living beings on this planet. Cohering one energy system for the highest good. While science supports what and how of the physical realm, consciousness allows right human actions to transcend ego drives, aligning humanity as a unified exemplary state of conscious expression for cooperation to expand. Humans are much more than physical; we are spiritual expressions of the conscious universal mind.

Similarly, the biofield is a highly organized subtle energy field around the body, connecting the body's other fields through entrainment. These geometric patterns are in constant contact with the quantum field, influencing it as it influences us. Epigenetics shows our perceptions in life govern this field of the human body.

Thoughts shrink or expand our field. Coherence of mind and body expands our field. Organized, positive, heartfelt thoughts connect our field to source energy greater than any other action, amplifying conductivity, and coherence in our immediate surroundings.

City dwellers naturally have smaller fields due to the incoherent environments. Practicing breathing, yoga, Qigong, and meditation supports a deeper coherence and is critical for anyone living in a congested area. Nature naturally opens our field into a larger expansive expression by relaxing our mental processes. Negative ions are responsible for this shift in chaotic thought patterns as nature is infused with negative ions.

The human body emits many frequencies via many fields, such as heart and brain magnetics, bions, infrared, etc. These cohered fields extend out of the body into the universal field with bions being the body's universal broadcast system. Bions connect the body to source energy.

Applying frequencies via light therapy is how I chose to help people feel better for the past twenty years. Applying laser light along meridian systems, organs, specific chakras, or plexus offers essential information in sequencing normal cell functions for energy levels to return.

Einstein knew the field was the governing agent. Connecting to the field via light infusions opens endless possibilities in the field of energy medicine. Coherent information shifts the body into dynamic states of vitality. Vibrating cells and atoms are picked up on modern super quantum imaging devices, yet these energy scans are read to utilize chemical solutions rather than energy modalities to rectify the variances found within the scans.

I had a client several years back who came to me when her mother was frustrated with the current medical experience. She was told her daughter was wasting away due to a hole leaking spinal fluid from the base of the spine. Headaches and weight loss would ensure the daughter wasted away and died.

This poor mother was devastated and had heard I do work with light. She came openhearted and allowed her daughter to experience a healing of sorts. I merely instilled the light of her cells into her meridian centers, upgrading her cellular communication back to normal cell functions. I intentionally held space for her to reconnect with her divine source light system.

This process took less than twenty minutes, yet I monitored her light sequencing for nearly an hour before releasing them from their session. The healing was a great success as the mother returned one month later to verify the light held and didn't require any additional coherence.

The modern medical model is changing with new technologies requiring a different vantage point in the business of medicine and health care. Infusing light, we influence chemical signals more efficiently than using chemistry alone.

Guidance by world-renowned geneticist and immunologist Dr. Peter Kay, I learned the importance of sequencing for specific protein production. The sequencing comes from the bion's light emission of the gene within each cell.

While I had great results helping people clear blocked energy patterns within their fields, allowing energy and vitality to return to normal, the time frame could be lengthy in getting lasting results. Applying intentional light-infusions took my practice to the next level. Light educates us on how amazing the human body, mind and spirit can truly be.

Light dims when we are stressed, via thoughts or structural patterns, changing our chemistry, oxygen levels, circulation, and ultimately our geometric patterns that connect us to source. Since more than 70 percent of negative thoughts are looped from redundancy, actively practicing accessing the creative conscious mind helps us illuminate our light body while reprogramming our body for life-affirming actions. The subconscious patterns of childhood no longer run our life. We choose to expand as we clear out old patterns of hurts that drain our energy and keep us locked into the past.

While talk therapies are ways to see the hurts, they tend to fail in offering solutions to resolve the hurts. Psychotherapy practices are advancing into energy psychology. No longer are we talking about the issue, reliving it in vivid detail repeatedly infusing our body with continuous biochemical stress patterns.

Energy tools coupled with neurolinguistic programing, movement, breathwork, and sequence-specific protein solutions support reprogramming the mind's chemistry and physiological matrix. Breaking out of old thought patterns is probably one of the most basic ways to restore vibrancy to a lethargic body system.

Emotions change the brain through unconscious stressors and reactions keeping us locked into energy drains. Releasing these drains through energy healing, light or touch therapies support long-term success. There are hundreds of items of evidence currently available on Google Scholar or WebMD supporting the benefits of energy healing. There's no need to cite any here. The truth is the body can regulate imbalances by accessing energy.

Energy travels at the speed of light or faster in some cases, which is why bions appear weak by modern instrument readings. Coherence of the entire body system into homeostasis can take minutes or hours, depending on the drains the practitioner is up against.

A homodynamic state is the perfect frequency of our cells, tissues, and organs vibrating in perfect pitch, tempo, and frequency for supreme expression of viable actions. Harmony.

Once a practitioner establishes this state within their subject, the coherent state holds or diminishes depending on the client's habitual tendencies. Energy patterns must be altered within all areas of mind, body, and spirit for long-term results to succeed.

Working the mind/body is inherent in where thoughts go, energy flows. The same is true for blood: where the blood flows, nutrients go, and flesh grows regeneratively. Keeping our mind still while moving our body is where coherence is often challenged. Aggressive competitive sports tend to wear out the body through extremes, stressing performance over coherence.

Gentle movement is what the centenarians teach us is best for longevity. Maintaining awareness of body structure when we stand, walk, and talk. Being mindful of the words we use, the tones, even our thoughts regulate our luminous field. Slowing our breathing process also enhances regenerative properties of the body. Breathing in slowly a little longer drawing in from the naval and exhaling fully elongates breath, diaphragm while expanding oxygenation and energy.

Deep, full breaths at a rate of a seven- or eight-second count uses less exertion to energize our cells. Since our breath changes our biofield, cohering breath often helps us access endless energy. Working with energy opens a new path for improving not only our health but also our lives.

This spontaneously uplifts those around us, affecting not only family but communities, regions, and nations. This is how we cohere a conscious global community. One deep breath at a time.

Everything begins with a creative thought. We have a choice to do harm or to rise out of primitive egocentric thought patterns initiated by competition and select harmonized collective conscious thoughts that raise others up.

Humanity's recycling of destructive thought patterns is at a pivotal time for review. Facing the war victims, we see these victims of hate crimes spread throughout our communities via gun violence.

Listening and truly hearing the stories of absurdity against human life touches my heart and higher self. I honestly believe our world will succeed in seeing the ugly truth of these crimes and rise above them to secure a peaceful future for all.

How are we as human beings entertaining harm when we know better? We've all experienced in some way or form the fallout of violence. Repeating these violent acts toward one another shows up in our collective whole as hate crimes as war proliferate the headlines. World leaders are characters playing out the deepest, darkest sides of our unconscious ego states.

Continuing to entertain destructive ego forces by identifying with primitive actions against one another will no doubt be the end of humanity. We are going backward, stuck in an unconscious loop, repeating destructive acts that no longer serve the greater good. Knowledge of our potential must be recognized for humanity to excel and grow into the luminous beings we are designed to be.

The universe is exposing the dark side of humanity for us to see the differences of who we are, where we've come from, and the possibilities of where we can go. The process of freedom and creativity based in fear deters life. It fails to honor a balanced decision to be made for humanity to flourish.

It is our choice as an individual, community, region, and country to choose higher expressions toward one another. The time is now to choose to live cooperatively. Harnessing 0.1 hertz for the well-being of our selves, community, and global community. Who's with me?

Getting to the root of humanity's traumatic pasts, the unspoken horrors we all know exist and continue to manipulate the masses into believing it's the only way. Humanity is stepping into a heightened awareness of knowing the difference in what feels right, 0.1 hertz, and what feels inhumanely deprecating to humanity at large. The old has fallen away as the new has already been formed and is thriving with innocence untouched by the darkness of humanity once lost.

The darkness often lives in addiction and unproductive actions toward self and others. This mania of sorts to have more, more, and more experiential moments gilded in kind are an illusion of men's making since the beginning of time. A look over here while we do this elsewhere. A mind that is fractal and barely aware. Caught in horror or even despair.

Traumatic experiences are often overlooked. The base of which is best spelled out by Hungarian Canadian professor Dr. Gabor Mate, whose compassionate inquiry has changed how we view trauma and more so how we treat it.

We each go through a human experience to help us grow. Having tools to explore, release, and nourish our heart and head supports healing the hurts of humanity. Mate is the teacher all young people should explore for comprehending the why of their actions. Also, practitioners will enhance their healing arts by learning his techniques. Breaking cycles of hurts that came from before, we empower humanity to be that much more.

A Few of My Favorites

There are many amazing teachers currently on the planet. A few of my favorites include the following:

- Gregg Braden, who has uncovered ancient wisdom hidden from humanity, bringing this knowledge forward in a very comprehensive way.
- Dr. Joe Dispenza, who made neuroscience and the unconscious mind easy to grasp while forging a global movement in meditation.
- Dr. Bruce Lipton, who grandfathered epigenetics into existence, proving environment distinguishes what we create, not our DNA.
- Louis Hay, who taught us that affirmations, our self-talk, can heal. She's living proof of that power.
- Heart Math Institute, which continues to expand the awareness of 0.1 hertz coherence of life.
- Resonance Science Organization, led by Nassim Haramein, who continues to prove that old perspectives of science no longer apply to our current state of awareness.
- Dr. Gabor Mate, who has revised how we see trauma in the body and how to heal it.

I could go on and on. The point is we are asking you to join forces, open your hearts, and consider a new paradigm. A world where life is supported no matter what color skin, hair, or eyes. We care about all beings, large and small, swimmers and flyers as well as those who walk and crawl. We honor and nurture the Earth for the gift of life it brings to every one of us.

We are asking all beings to become the luminous creative expression of our collective divine self, cohered in one universal field. One coherent unified human race.

It's Time. Who's with me?

Printed in the United States
by Baker & Taylor Publisher Services

essentials

Essentials liefern aktuelles Wissen in konzentrierter Form. Die Essenz dessen, worauf es als „State-of-the-Art" in der gegenwärtigen Fachdiskussion oder in der Praxis ankommt. Essentials informieren schnell, unkompliziert und verständlich

- als Einführung in ein aktuelles Thema aus Ihrem Fachgebiet
- als Einstieg in ein für Sie noch unbekanntes Themenfeld
- als Einblick, um zum Thema mitreden zu können.

Die Bücher in elektronischer und gedruckter Form bringen das Expertenwissen von Springer-Fachautoren kompakt zur Darstellung. Sie sind besonders für die Nutzung als eBook auf Tablet-PCs, eBook-Readern und Smartphones geeignet.

Essentials: Wissensbausteine aus Wirtschaft und Gesellschaft, Medizin, Psychologie und Gesundheitsberufen, Technik und Naturwissenschaften. Von renommierten Autoren der Verlagsmarken Springer Gabler, Springer VS, Springer Medizin, Springer Spektrum, Springer Vieweg und Springer Psychologie.

Thomas Deelmann

Managementberatung in Deutschland

Grundlagen, Trends, Prognosen

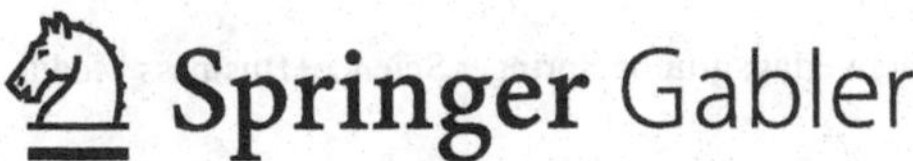

Prof. Dr. Thomas Deelmann
BiTS Iserlohn
Deutschland

ISSN 2197-6708 ISSN 2197-6716 (electronic)
essentials
ISBN 978-3-658-08891-0 ISBN 978-3-658-08892-7 (eBook)
DOI 10.1007/978-3-658-08892-7

Die Deutsche Nationalbibliothek verzeichnet diese Publikation in der Deutschen Nationalbibliografie; detaillierte bibliografische Daten sind im Internet über http://dnb.d-nb.de abrufbar.

Springer Gabler

Gedruckt auf säurefreiem und chlorfrei gebleichtem Papier

Springer Fachmedien Wiesbaden ist Teil der Fachverlagsgruppe Springer Science+Business Media (www.springer.com)

Was Sie in diesem Essential finden können

- Einen Überblick zu idealtypischen Beratungsformen und -feldern sowie eine Darstellung der Entwicklung des Branchenumsatzes.
- Hintergrundgedanken zu aktuell sichtbaren und möglichen zukünftigen Trends der Beratung.
- Insgesamt elf Thesen aus sechs Themenfeldern zur Branchensituation.
- Persönliche Bewertungen und Kommentierungen von 14 ausgewiesenen Fachexperten zu den gestellten Thesen.
- Eine konsolidierte Einschätzung der Einzelaussagen und dadurch insgesamt einen exzellenten Einblick in die Managementberatungsszene – und ihre voraussichtliche Entwicklung!

Vorwort

Akademische Arbeiten und populäre Literatur zur Managementberatung sind auf Grund des Angebots- und Nachfragebooms in den letzten Jahren beziehungsweise Jahrzehnten zwar keine Ausnahme mehr, allerdings auch noch nicht die Regel. Forschungsaktivitäten und Publikationen zu diesem Thema scheinen dem Empfinden des Verfassers nach temporären und örtlichen Häufungen zu unterliegen – es kann vom Vorhandensein verschiedener Forschungsinseln gesprochen werden. Diese Einzelarbeiten sind wichtig und nicht zu vernachlässigen. Jedoch sollte durchaus Ziel einer aufstrebenden Wissenschaftsdomäne sein, die einzelnen Beiträge miteinander zu verbinden und Verknüpfungen herzustellen.

Kern bzw. Ausgangspunkt des vorliegenden Beitrages ist es, eine zeitliche Brücke zu einer gut zehn Jahre zurückliegenden Betrachtung unter dem Titel „Beratung: Quo vadis“ sowie den sich ihr anschließenden Ausführungen, die an anderer Stelle erschienen sind, zu schlagen und den Versuch einer aktuelle Zustandsbeschreibung und eines Ausblicks zu wagen. Hierzu sind im Rahmen einer Expertenbefragung verschiedene Thesen zur Diskussion gestellt und teilweise kontrovers diskutiert worden. Neben einer Zustandsbeschreibung wird dadurch auch die Skizzierung einer Zukunftsperspektive möglich.

Sehr herzlich möchte der Verfasser daher den Teilnehmern an der Delphi-Studie „Managementberatung in Deutschland“ danken, ohne deren Unterstützung, Auskunftsbereitschaft und Einschätzungen die vorliegende Studie nicht ihr Diskussionspotenzial und ihre Aussagekraft erhalten hätte!

Iserlohn, Januar 2015 Thomas Deelmann

Inhaltsverzeichnis

1 Einleitung . . . 1
1.1 Motivation . . . 1
1.2 Ziel . . . 2
1.3 Aufbau . . . 2

2 Grundlagen . . . 3
2.1 Beratung . . . 3
2.2 Beratungsmarkt . . . 5
2.3 Beratungsfelder . . . 5
2.4 Beratungsformen . . . 7
2.5 Anbieterstruktur . . . 9

3 Studiendesign . . . 11
3.1 Methodik . . . 11
3.2 Studienteilnehmer . . . 11
3.3 Ergebnisdarstellung . . . 13

4 Konvergenz von Beratungsgeschäftsfeldern . . . 15
4.1 Einführung . . . 15
4.2 These 1 („Konvergenz“) . . . 15
4.3 Ergebnisse . . . 16
4.4 Bewertung . . . 18

5 Automatisierung von Beratungsleistungen . . . 19
5.1 Einführung . . . 19
5.2 These 2 („Automatisierung“) . . . 19
5.3 Ergebnisse . . . 20
5.4 Bewertung . . . 21

6 Reifegrad der Beratungsindustrie 23
6.1 Einführung 23
6.2 These 3 („Reife“) 23
6.3 Ergebnisse 23
6.4 Bewertung 25

7 Relevanz des deutschen Beratungsmarktes im internationalen Kontext 27
7.1 Einführung 27
7.2 These 4 („Relevanz“) 27
7.3 Ergebnisse 28
7.4 Bewertung 29

8 Explizit artikulierte und nicht explizit artikulierte Beratungsbedarfe 31
8.1 Einführung 31
8.2 These 5 („Bedarfe“) 31
8.3 Ergebnisse 32
8.4 Bewertung 33

9 Office-Dichte der großen Strategieberatungen in Deutschland 35
9.1 Einführung 35
9.2 These 6.1 („Auf den Grund gehen“) 35
9.3 Ergebnisse 36
9.4 Bewertung 36
9.5 These 6.2 („Managementstil“) 37
9.6 Ergebnisse 37
9.7 Bewertung 38
9.8 These 6.3 („Rollentausch“) 38
9.9 Ergebnisse 38
9.10 Bewertung 40
9.11 These 6.4 („Obrigkeits-Bejahung“) 40
9.12 Ergebnisse 40
9.13 Bewertung 42
9.14 These 6.5 („Klientenprofessionalisierung“) 42
9.15 Ergebnisse 42
9.16 Bewertung 43
9.17 These 6.6 („Dezentrale Wirtschaftsstruktur“) 44
9.18 Ergebnisse 44
9.19 Bewertung 45

10 Abschluss 47
10.1 Zusammenfassung 47
10.2 Fazit 48
10.3 Ausblick 49

Was Sie aus diesem Essential mitnehmen können 51

Literatur 53

Einleitung 1

1.1 Motivation

Das Angebot von und die Nachfrage nach Unternehmensberatungsleistungen[1] sind in den vergangenen Jahren deutlich angestiegen. Das Marktwachstum hat das Wachstum anderer Branchen deutlich übertroffen und Unternehmensberatungen werden in Umfragen unter Studierenden und Berufseinsteigern zu den beliebtesten Arbeitgebern gezählt. Dieser positiven Einschätzung wird aber regelmäßig auch Kritik an der Branche oder einzelner Branchenvertreter entgegengestellt.

Zudem scheint der deutsche Beratungsmarkt bzw. die Beratung in Deutschland im internationalen Vergleich eine gewisse Attraktivität aufzuweisen: So stammten bzw. stammen in der jüngeren Vergangenheit führende Manager der großen Strategieberatungen aus Deutschland. Zudem ist die absolute Anzahl ihrer Büros (Niederlassungen) in Deutschland mit 28 (nach den USA mit 57) die zweithöchste der Welt.

Mit der Inanspruchnahme von Beratungsleistungen verfolgen Kundenunternehmen oft das Ziel, Unsicherheit zu reduzieren. Bei in die Zukunft gerichteten Fragestellungen können Berater direkten Rat geben, Hilfe zur Selbsthilfe aussprechen oder den Kunden durch Irritationen zum Nachdenken bewegen.

[1] Besser wäre der Gebrauch des Terms *Organisationale Beratung* (s. u.), da neben Unternehmen auch Behörden und andere Organisationen die Dienstleistung in Anspruch nehmen. Im Sprachgebrauch hat sich jedoch *Unternehmensberatung* durchgesetzt; dieser Entwicklung wird hier i. W. gefolgt.

T. Deelmann, *Managementberatung in Deutschland,* essentials,
DOI 10.1007/978-3-658-08892-7_1

Wenig intensiv diskutiert werden allerdings Fragen zur Zukunft der Beratung, ihrer Funktion und ihrer Interaktion mit den Kunden, z. B.:

- Wie und ob sich Berater mit einer Automatisierung ihrer eigenen Branche auseinander setzen;
- Wie sie auf ein verändertes Nachfrageverhalten ihrer Kunden reagieren;
- Ob es eine Tendenz zu mehr Transparenz und Offenheit bei ihrer impliziten und expliziten Aufgabe in Kundenorganisationen gibt?

1.2 Ziel

Vor diesem Hintergrund hat die Delphi-Studie „Managementberatung in Deutschland" das Ziel, ausgewählte Thesen zu diesem Komplex zur Diskussion stellen.

14 Experten[2] (davon 5 Teilnehmer aus Beratungs- und 4 aus Kundenunternehmen sowie 5 Marktbeobachter) haben im Juli und August 2014 ihre Zustimmung oder Ablehnung zu sechs Themenfeldern mit insgesamt elf Thesen ausgedrückt und die Thesen umfangreich kommentiert. Die Ergebnisse der Studie werden im vorliegenden Beitrag zusammengefasst.

1.3 Aufbau

Hierfür werden nach diesem einleitenden Abschnitt im folgenden zweiten Kapitel zunächst begriffliche Grundlagen gelegt und der Beratungsmarkt u. a. an Hand seiner Volumenentwicklung sowie der vorhandenen Beratungsfelder und -formen beschrieben.

Im dritten Kapitel wird das Studiendesign kurz vorgestellt und in den sich anschließenden Kapiteln stehen die einzelnen Thesen im Mittelpunkt. Dabei wird zunächst jeweils der gedankliche Hintergrund für die Aufstellung einer These skizziert, dann wird die These selber expliziert und die Zustimmung bzw. Ablehnung der befragten Experten wird dargestellt. Diese Darstellung erfolgt summarisch und in Form vorhandener Kommentare, bevor eine abschließende kurze Bewertung gegeben wird.

Ein abschließendes zehntes Kapitel fasst die Inhalte des vorliegenden Beitrages schließlich nochmal zusammen, zieht ein Fazit und bietet einen kleinen Ausblick auf weitere, sich anschließende Forschungsfragen.

[2] Rein aus Gründen der Lesbarkeit wird in dieser Unterlage i. d. R. die männliche Form verwendet, wobei das weibliche Geschlecht gleichermaßen gemeint ist.

Grundlagen

2

2.1 Beratung

Für die vorliegende Arbeit wird auf folgende Arbeitsdefinition von Beratung zurückgegriffen:[1]

> Als organisationale Beratung wird ein professioneller, vertraglich beauftragter Dienstleistungs- und Transformationsprozess der intervenierenden Begleitung durch ein Beratersystem bei der Analyse, Beschreibung und Lösung eines Problems des Kundensystems – i. S. einer Arbeit an Entscheidungsprämissen – mit dem Ziel der Transformation verstanden.

Die einzelnen Aspekte der Definition im Detail:

- *Professionalität:* Mit diesem Kriterium wird Beratung in dem hier verstanden Sinne von einer irgendwie geartete Hilfestellung oder Unterstützung abgegrenzt.
- *Vertragliche Beauftragung:* Ist als ein formales Kriterium zentral, da sie die Beziehung zwischen Beratung und Kunde initialisiert und sich – auch innerorganisatorisch – von einem einfachen Anweisungsverhältnis im Rahmen bestehender

[1] mit kleineren semantischen und orthographischen Anpassungen entnommen aus: Deelmann et al. (2006, S. 6–7).

T. Deelmann, *Managementberatung in Deutschland,* essentials,
DOI 10.1007/978-3-658-08892-7_2

Arbeitsverträge abhebt. Das Arbeitsverhältnis ist ein systematisch unvollständiger Vertrag.

- *Prozess:* Organisationale Beratung wird – auch in interaktionsarmen Beratungstypen wie der Gutachterberatung – als Prozess verstanden und grenzt sich so von singulären „Ereignissen", wie einmalige Vorträgen, Weiterbildungsveranstaltungen oder Gesprächen ab.
- *Intervenierende Begleitung*: Damit ist ein offener Oberbegriff für im Hinblick auf die Interventionen zu unterscheidenden Typen der Beratung bezeichnet, der verschiedene Interventionen wie gutachterliche Beratung, Expertenberatung oder systemische Beratung umfasst. Der Begriff der „Begleitung" grenzt sich von anderen Formen der Zusammenarbeit (z. B. Co-Management) oder ersetzender Arbeit (Interimsmanagement) ab.
- *Beratersystem*: Damit wird ein abgegrenztes System – bestehend aus einer oder mehrerer Personen und deren Interaktionsbeziehungen – bezeichnet, das nicht identisch mit dem Kundensystem ist. Im Falle der Externen Beratung ist dies bereits durch eine gesellschaftsrechtlich und wirtschaftlich eigenständige Entität gegeben. Im Falle der Internen Beratung sind hingegen Grenzziehungen in einer Binnenstruktur einer Organisation zentral (i.e.S. einer Abteilung). Wesentlich dabei ist die fehlende direkte Betroffenheit des Beratersystems von einem Problem des Kundensystems – wenngleich eine in-direkte Verbundenheit besteht.
- *Analyse, Beschreibung und Lösung*: Damit sind die Aufgaben der Beratung beschrieben, wobei hier darauf hingewiesen werden muss, dass grundsätzlich eine Informationsasymmetrie zugunsten des Kunden vorliegt, so dass die Beratung mehr zur Hervorbringung sowie zur Irritation von Selbstbeschreibungen von Problemen und Lösungen des Kundensystems – i. S. einer sokratischen Mäeutik – beitragen muss, als auf Basis eines bloßen Umweltwissen bereits Empfehlungen zu geben.
- *Problem des Kundensystems*: Damit wird betont, dass es nicht um von dem Beratersystem – möglicherweise ausgehend von der verfügbaren Lösung – projizierte Probleme gehen kann, die vom Kunden zu lösen sind, sondern um eine gemeinsame Erarbeitung von Lösungen für virulente Probleme des Kunden.
- *Arbeit an Entscheidungsprämissen*: Der Kunde ist der einzige, der in der Berater-Kunden-Beziehung für die Kundenorganisation entscheiden kann. Beratung trägt zur Vergegenwärtigung, Evaluierung und ggf. Veränderung von in der Vergangenheit bereits entschiedenen Entscheidungen bzw. Entscheidungsprämissen bei. Damit ist aber auch der wesentliche Unterschied zwischen – sowohl Externer wie Interner – Beratung und dem Kunde bezeichnet: Die riskante Entscheidung – unter Unsicherheit – trifft einzig der Kunde. Und zwar auch dann, wenn dies auf der Grundlage eines mehr oder minder starken Einflusses durch Berater geschieht. Im Gegensatz zu Externen Beratungen können sich die Fol-

gen von ‚schlechter Beratung' allerdings auch auf die weiteren Bedingungen der Möglichkeit ‚Interner Beratung' nachhaltiger auswirken, da in der Regel zwischen Interner Beratungseinheit und Mutterorganisation ein direkterer Legitimations- und Finanzierungszusammenhang besteht.

- *Transformation*: Beratung hat das Ziel, dass in dem Klientensystem eine neue Form im Sinne einer Selbstveränderung des Kundensystems gefunden werden kann.

2.2 Beratungsmarkt

Unternehmensberatungsleistungen erfreuen sich insbesondere in Deutschland einer hohen Beliebtheit. So liegt beispielsweise das Marktwachstums regelmäßig sichtbar über dem gesamtwirtschaftlichen Wachstum. Gleichzeitig wird allerdings auch regelmäßig (teilweise polemisch und pointiert) deutliche Kritik geäußert.

Zudem scheint der deutsche Beratungsmarkt bzw. die Beratung in Deutschland im internationalen Vergleich eine gewissen Attraktivität aufzuweisen: So stammen bzw. stammten in der jüngeren Vergangenheit führende Manager der großen Strategieberatungen aus Deutschland. Zudem ist die absolute Anzahl ihrer Büros (Niederlassungen) in Deutschland mit 28 (nach den USA mit 57) die zweithöchste der Welt.

Abbildung 2.1 zeigt die Entwicklung des Marktvolumens von 1980 bis heute auf. Im langfristigen Durchschnitt ist der Markt jährlich um 8,4 % gewachsen, kurzfristige Rückgänge waren lediglich dreimal (1993, 2002–2003 sowie 2009) zu verzeichnen.

Neben der reinen Volumenbetrachtung kann der Markt unter anderem auch nach der Verteilung der im Schwerpunkt genutzten Beratungsformen und der Beratungsinhalte, ausgedrückt durch die Beratungsfelder betrachtet werden.

2.3 Beratungsfelder

Das *Beratungsfeld* beschreibt dabei eine oder mehrere funktionale Kompetenzausprägungen des Beratersystems. Als Funktionen bzw. als Beratungsfeld unterscheidet der Bundesverband Deutscher Unternehmensberater BDU e. V. die Strategieberatung, die Organisations- und Prozessberatung, HR-Beratung und IT-Beratung. Eine Abgrenzung wird dort nicht beschreibend, sondern enumerativ mit Hilfe von Unterklassen gegeben. Grundsätzlich ist anzumerken, dass die einzelnen Beratungsfelder sich als nicht scharf abgegrenzt präsentieren, sondern durch die Reputation der jeweils prominentesten Branchenvertreter geprägt und ausgestaltet

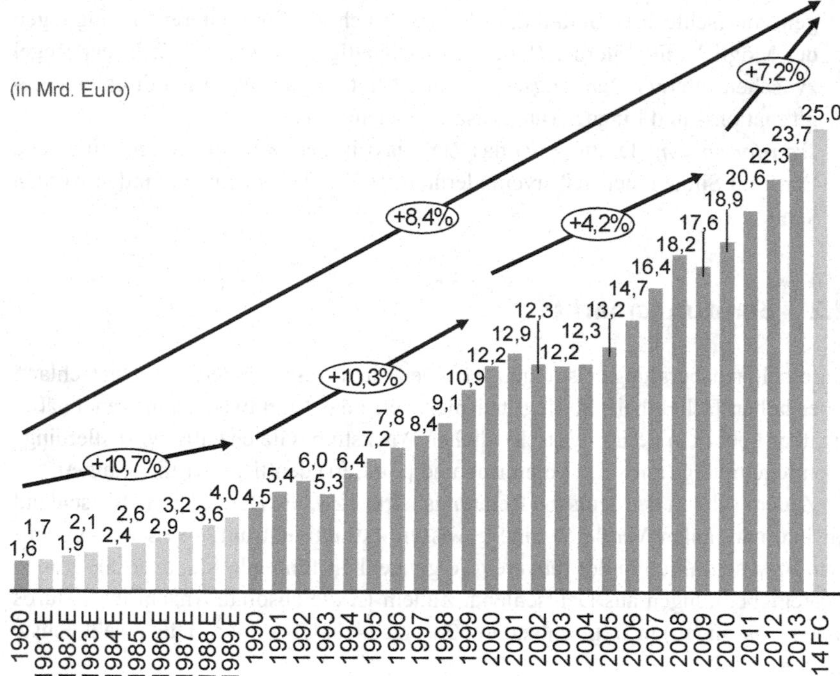

Abb. 2.1 Volumen und Zusammensetzung des Beratungsmarktes in Deutschland. (Marktdaten sind i. W. verschiedenen Publikationen des BDU, vgl. BDU (2014) und Vorgängerpublikationen, entnommen. Für 1981–1989 sind durch den Verfasser geschätzte Werte (E, estimate) und für 2014 Prognosewerte (FC, forecast) angegeben. Die Prozentwerte stellen die durchschnittlichen jährlichen Wachstumsraten für die entsprechenden Perioden dar)

werden. Sie haben sich historisch zur heute gebräuchlichen Abgrenzung hin entwickelt und werden sich voraussichtlich auch zukünftig weiterentwickeln.

Im Einzelnen hat die *Strategieberatung* das Ziel, langfristige und strategische Verbesserungen, oftmals mit fundamentalem Charakter, in einer Organisation herbeizuführen. Beispiele sind die strategische Planung oder Restrukturierungen. Der BDU schätzt für die jüngere Vergangenheit, dass circa ein Viertel des Marktvolumens auf die Strategieberatung entfällt. *Organisations- und Prozessberatung* hat das Ziel, operative Aspekte einer Organisation zu verbessern. Als Beispiele können hier Änderungen an Geschäftsprozessen, Organisationsmaßnahmen oder Change Management-Initiativen genannt werden. Dieses Beratungsfeld stellt mit knapp 45 % das größte Marktsegment. *HR-Beratung* zielt darauf ab, das „menschliche"

Element bzw. den Einsatz des menschlichen (Produktions-) Faktors in der Organisation zu verbessern. Beispiele sind Recruiting oder HR-Development-Maßnahmen. Gut 10 % des Beratungsmarktes lassen sich hier einordnen. *IT-Beratung* schließlich versucht den Umgang mit Daten und Informationen, d. h. ihre Gewinnung, Speicherung, Verarbeitung, Ausgabe und Nutzung, zu verbessern. Beispiele für die Verbesserung des Umgangs mit Informationstechnologie im Unternehmen sind IT-Architektur-Management-Projekte und umfangreichere Programmwartungsaktivitäten. Auf dieses Beratungsfeld entfallen gut 20 % des Gesamtmarktes.

Im Rahmen der durchgeführten Studie wurde auf die beiden Felder Strategie- sowie Organisations- und Prozessberatung fokussiert. Ihnen wurde als Oberbegriff Managementberatung zugewiesen und sie decken mit gut zwei Dritteln den Großteil des Marktes ab.[2]

Die Verteilung des Marktes auf die einzelnen Beratungsfelder ist in den vergangenen circa 10 Jahren für die HR-Beratung relativ konstant bei circa 10 % geblieben. Auch die Strategieberatung deckt kontinuierlich circa ein Viertel des Marktes ab, hatte aber zuletzt 2005–2006 ein kleines Zwischenhoch. Die größte Veränderung in der relativen Marktaufteilung ist zwischen der IT-Beratung und der Organisations- und Prozessberatung zu beobachten. Die IT-Beratung hat zur Jahrtausendwende noch fast die Hälfte des Beratungsmarktes umfasst. Während der letzten Dekade ist ihr Anteil von dann gut 29 auf gut 21 % geschrumpft. Die Organisations- und Prozessberatung konnte ihren Anteil am Gesamtmarkt hingegen von circa einem Drittel auf deutlich über zwei Fünftel erhöhen. Abbildung 2.2 stellt die Zusammensetzung des Marktes im Zeitverlauf nochmal grafisch dar.

2.4 Beratungsformen

Als *Beratungsform* oder *Interventionsform* wird im Folgenden die durch den Interaktionsgrad geprägte Herangehensweise an eine Beratungsintervention verstanden. Die gewählte Beratungsform determiniert deutlich das Vorgehen und Zusammenwirken zwischen Berater und Beratenem. Es lassen sich vier idealtypische Beratungsformen unterscheiden:[3]

Gutachterliche Beratung: Die gutachterliche Beratung interpretiert eine Organisation als reines Mittel zu einer Zielrealisierung. „In diesem Kontext heißt

[2] Vgl. BDU (2014, S. 21) für eine Beschreibung der Beratungsfelder (wobei dort entgegen der obigen Zusammenfassung der Begriff Managementberatung weiter definiert wird) und S. 9 für die Marktanteile.

[3] Vgl. für die folgende Beschreibung der vier Beratungsformen Walger (1995).

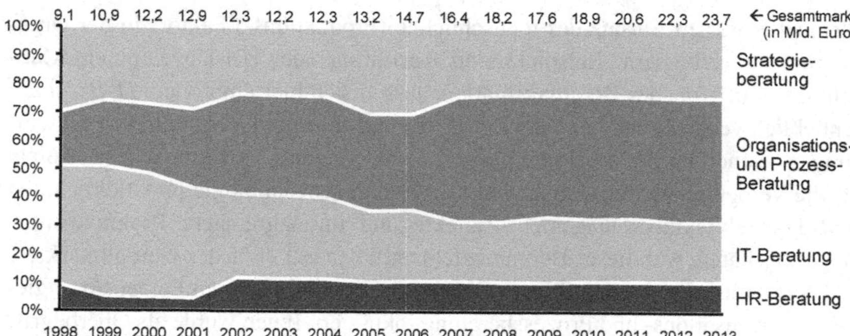

Abb. 2.2 Zusammensetzung des Beratungsmarktes in Deutschland im Zeitverlauf. (Vgl. BDU (2014, S. 9) und Vorgängerpublikationen)

Beratung, Informationen zu beschaffen und Alternativen zu bewerten [… sowie] Antwort auf gestellte Fragen zu geben, die der Vorbereitung einer Entscheidung dient.“

Expertenberatung: Bei der Expertenberatung wird die Organisation als ein sozio-technisches System sowie als offene Organisation verstanden. Mitarbeiter von Berater- und Klientensystem arbeiten gemeinsam auf die Lösung eines gegebenen Problems hin.

Organisationsentwicklung Leitbild der Organisationsentwicklung ist die lernende Organisation. Der Berater reflektiert den Beratenen und bietet so Hilfe zur Selbsthilfe an.

Systemische Beratung Die systemische Beratung definiert eine Organisation über die Grenzen zur jeweiligen Umwelt sowie über die jeweiligen internen Zusammenhänge von Funktionen. Berater reflektieren hierbei nicht mehr den Beratenen, wie noch bei der Organisationsentwicklung, sondern versuchen der zu beratenen Organisation eine Selbstreflektion zu ermöglichen. Wesentlich ist hierbei die sog. Irritation des Kundensystems durch den Berater.

Die oben gewählte Reihenfolge orientiert sich zum einen an einem zunehmenden Grad der Interaktion zwischen Berater und Beratenem sowie einer für den Berater abnehmenden Notwendigkeit, das Umfeld des Kunden, also z. B. Branchen- oder Organisationsdetails, zu kennen. In der Praxis sind sowohl diese vier idealtypischen Beratungsformen sowie Mischformen hieraus anzutreffen.

Es wird geschätzt, dass die Form der Expertenberatung dabei mit 85 % den größten Umfang einnimmt, gefolgt von der Organisationsentwicklung (11 %) und der systemischen sowie gutachterlichen Beratung (jeweils circa 2 %).

2.5 Anbieterstruktur

In 2013 gab es 15.300 Beratungsunternehmen, die mit 98.250 Beratern einen Umsatz von 23,7 Mrd. € erwirtschaftet haben. Neben den Beratern haben die Beratungsunternehmen weitere 24.250 Mitarbeiter in Nicht-Beraterrollen beschäftigt. Dies führt zu einer durchschnittlichen Overhead-Quote von 20 %.

Werden die Beratungsunternehmen nach ihrer Umsatzgröße differenziert betrachtet, so fällt auf, dass die 150 großen Beratungshäuser, d. h. Unternehmen mit einem Umsatz von 45 Mio. € oder mehr pro Jahr, einen Marktanteil von über 43 % aufweisen. Dies sind 10,2 Mrd. €. Sie erzielen mit 32.000 Beratern einen durchschnittlichen Umsatz von 319.000 € pro Jahr und Berater. Die numerisch stärkste Größenklasse ist die der sehr kleinen Beratungsunternehmen (oft vermutlich auch Einzelunternehmer). Hier gibt es 7.800 Unternehmen mit 13.000 Beratern (durchschnittlicher Umsatz pro Berater: 122.000 € pro Jahr) und einem Marktanteil von 6,7 % bzw. einen Gesamtumsatz von 1,6 Mrd. €.

Wird der Fokus auf die zehn größten Managementberatungsunternehmen gelegt, so fällt auf, dass ihr Marktanteil in den vergangenen Jahren geschrumpft ist, die Marktkonzentration also nachgelassen hat. Das Umsatzvolumen der jeweils zehn größten Managementberatungen hat von 2002 bis 2012 um jährlich durchschnittlich 3,87 % zugenommen. Das Volumen des gesamten Marktes für Managementberatungsleistungen ist in dieser Zeit jedoch um jährlich durchschnittlich 7,69 % gewachsen und auch der Gesamtberatungsmarkt ist um durchschnittlich 6,13 % angestiegen.[4]

[4] Vgl. nochmal BDU (2014, S. 4–9) (und die Vorgängerpublikationen) für die Datengrundlage zum Gesamtmarkt und die sog. Lünendonk-Listen für die Datengrundlage der zehn größten Managementberatungsunternehmen.

Studiendesign

3

3.1 Methodik

Die Studie „Managementberatung in Deutschland“ wurde im Juli und August 2014 durch den Verfasser als sog. Delphi-Studie durchgeführt. Bei einer Delphi-Studie werden Experten in einem ersten Schritt um eine Einschätzung zu Thesen aus ihrem Fachgebiet gebeten. Die Einschätzungen werden anschließend konsolidiert (und anonymisiert) wieder an die Studienteilnehmer zurückgegeben. Diese haben nun die Möglichkeit, ihre eigene Einschätzung vor dem Hintergrund der Antworten der übrigen Fachexperten zu überdenken und gegebenenfalls anzupassen. Die Anzahl der Iterationen lässt sich beliebig wiederholen; Ziel ist es, durch mehrere Befragungsrunden eine höhere Validität der Antworten zu erhalten und zu einem Konsens zu gelangen.

Die durchgeführte Studie umfasste zwei Befragungsrunden und es wurden sechs Themen mit insgesamt elf Thesen zur Diskussion gestellt. Die Experten wurden gebeten, ihre Zustimmung oder Ablehnung zu einer These auf einer 5er-Skala zu artikulieren. Zusätzlich hatten sie die Möglichkeit, Kommentare als Freitext zu ergänzen.

3.2 Studienteilnehmer

14 Experten haben an der Studie teilgenommen, davon fünf Berater, vier Teilnehmer aus Kundenunternehmen und fünf Marktbeobachter. Die Berater gehörten alle dem Partner-Level (im Gegensatz zur Ebene Projektleiter oder Consultant) an.

T. Deelmann, *Managementberatung in Deutschland,* essentials,
DOI 10.1007/978-3-658-08892-7_3

- **Delphi-Studie mit zwei Befragungsrunden**
  - 6 Themen mit insgesamt 11 Thesen
  - Einschätzungen auf 5er-Skala und Freitext
  - Studienzeitraum: Juli und August 2014
- **Teilnehmer**
  - Anzahl: 14 Fachexperten
  - Zusammensetzung:

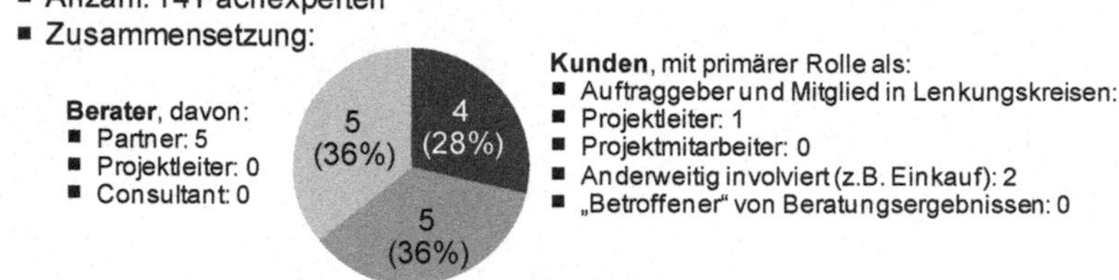

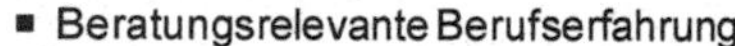

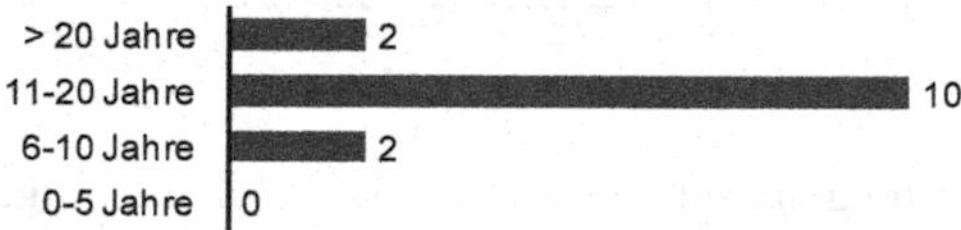

Abb. 3.1 Studiendesign im Überblick

Die Kunden sahen ihre primäre Rolle als Auftraggeber und Mitglied in Lenkungskreisen (ein Teilnehmer), als Projektleiter (ein Teilnehmer) oder als anderweitig Involvierter (zwei Teilnehmer), z. B. als Einkäufer. Die primäre Rolle des Projektmitarbeiters oder lediglich als Betroffener von Beratungsergebnissen hatte keiner inne. Zu der Gruppe der Marktbeobachter gehörten beispielsweise Journalisten oder Wissenschaftler mit einem Arbeitsschwerpunkt Beratung.

Zwei Teilnehmer gaben an, über eine beratungsrelevante Berufserfahrung von mehr als 20 Jahren zu verfügen, zehn über eine Erfahrung von 11–20 Jahre und zwei über eine Erfahrung von 6–10 Jahre zu verfügen. Abbildung 3.1 fasst das Studiendesign zusammen.

Nicht explizit abgefragt wurden Eigenangaben der Berater über ihre präferierte bzw. typischerweise angewendete Beratungsform. Aus Sicht des Verfassers können vier Teilnehmer in das Cluster der Expertenberatung (teilweise mit Sympathien zur Organisationsentwicklung) eingeordnet werden und ein Teilnehmer favorisiert die Beratungsform der Organisationsentwicklung, mit Anlehnungen zur systemischen Beratung. Damit wird der oben angesprochene Marktschnitt recht gut gespiegelt.

3.3 Ergebnisdarstellung

Die Studienergebnisse werden im Folgenden präsentiert. Zu jeder These werden zunächst einige Gedanken zum Hintergrund vorgestellt, anschließend die These selber und das jeweilige summarische Teilergebnis der Delphi-Studie aus der zweiten Runde präsentiert. Es erscheint hilfreich, auch die Kommentare der Studienteilnehmer wörtlich, aber anonym wiederzugeben, da hierin sowohl die Stimmung, als auch die Begründung für einzelne Wertungen reflektiert wird. Dabei wurden durch den Verfasser offensichtliche orthografische Fehler korrigiert und kleinere stilistische Eingriffe vorgenommen. Die Präsentation eines Themenfeldes bzw. einer These wird durch eine kurze Kommentierung und Bewertung abgeschlossen.

4 Konvergenz von Beratungsgeschäftsfeldern

4.1 Einführung

Prüfungsnahe Beratungsunternehmen haben in der jüngsten Vergangenheit Managementberatungsunternehmen gekauft, parallel bauen Strategieberatungen ihre IT-Kompetenz sichtbar aus und große IT-Beratungshäuser versuchen regelmäßig zunächst in die Felder Prozess- und Organisationsberatung und dann Strategieberatung vorzudringen.

Gleichzeitig melden sich Stimmen, die eine ausdifferenzierte Wettbewerbslandschaft präferieren und einer Angleichung der Geschäftsmodelle widersprechen.

Als Proxy für eine solche Geschäftsmodellkonvergenz oder -divergenz der Beratungsanbieter kann bspw. die Angleichung von Honoraren, Gehältern sowie dem Verhältnis von Partnern zu Beratern herangezogen werden.

4.2 These 1 („Konvergenz")

Die Geschäftsmodelle verschiedener Beratungsfelder (Strategie, Organisation & Prozesse, IT) werden sich in den kommenden fünf Jahren so stark angleichen, dass eine Unterscheidung beim größten Teil der Anbieter nur schwer möglich ist.

T. Deelmann, *Managementberatung in Deutschland,* essentials,
DOI 10.1007/978-3-658-08892-7_4

4.3 Ergebnisse

Die einzelnen Teilnehmer haben wie folgt Punkte von 5 („Der These stimme ich absolut zu!“) bis 1 („Der These stimme ich überhaupt nicht zu!“) vergeben:

2, 3, 3, 2, 1, 3, 3, 3, 4, 5, 3, 2, 1, 2. Das arithmetische Mittel beträgt *2,6*. Abbildung 4.1 stellt die Antworten nochmal grafisch dar.

Die Teilnehmer haben zusätzlich folgende *eher zustimmende Kommentare* abgegeben:

- „s. mein angehängter […] Aufsatz…“
  [In dem referenzierten Beitrag wird ausgeführt, dass i) IT-Dienstleister in das Segment der Organisations- und Prozessberatung streben, ii) klassische Strategieberater in Richtung IT-Beratung vorzudringen versuchen, iii) Full Service Provider das komplette Spektrum von Strategie- bis zu IT-Dienstleistungen anbieten wollen und iv) IT-Berater danach streben, sowohl Prozess-, als auch Strategieberatung anzubieten. (Seite 3–4 des Beitrags)
  Eine in diesem Beitrag veröffentlichte Praktikerumfrage zeichnet mit 58 % Zustimmung ein gemischtes Bild mit Blick auf die These „In jüngerer Vergangenheit erwarten die Beratungsklienten vermehrt eine Dienstleistung, welche die strategische Konzeption, das Prozessdesign und die IT-gestützte Implementierung, also den gesamten Prozess bis hin zur Umsetzung aus einer Hand umfasst.“ (Seite 9) D. Verf.]
- „Im Markt werden circa 2–3 Topmanagement-Berater ein eher vorstands- beziehungsweise aufsichtsratsorientiertes Geschäft machen. Für die meisten anderen würde ich der These zustimmen.“

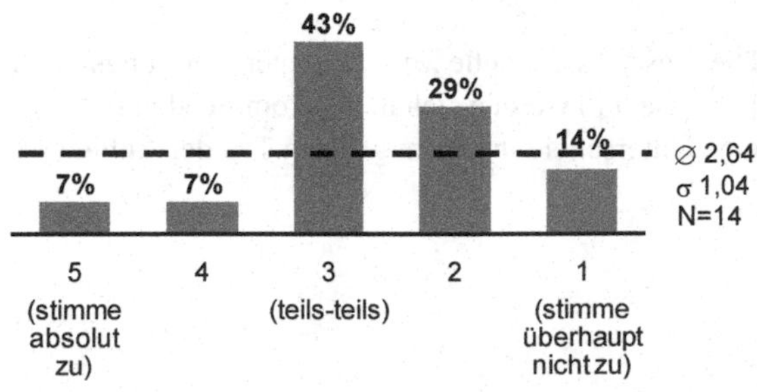

Abb. 4.1 Ergebnisdarstellung zur These der Konvergenz von Beratungsfeldern

- „Das wird für einige gelten – der Transformationsprozess insgesamt dauert wahrscheinlich länger."

Die Teilnehmer haben zusätzlich folgende *eher ablehnende Kommentare* abgegeben:

- „Beobachtet wird ja nicht eine notwendigerweise Angleichung der Geschäftsmodelle, sondern die Tendenz zur Vertiefung der Wertschöpfung bzw. Verbreiterung der Produktpalette, je nachdem, ob man das Produkt als „Veränderung des Unternehmens" definiert oder als „Beratung zur Strategie", „Beratung zur Organisation", „Beratung zur IT". Dass sich deshalb die Geschäftsmodelle (als Wertschöpfungskonzept) angleichen, erscheint mir nicht zwingend. Jedenfalls erfüllt diese Wertschöpfungsvertiefung unterschiedliche Zwecke bei den einzelnen Beratungen. Die Beratungen scheinen auch ihr Bouquet an neben einander bestehenden Geschäftsmodellen zu erweitern."
- „Zwar werden die Projekte, insbes. die größeren, immer stärker eine Vernetzung aller o. g. Themen mit sich bringen (z. B. von der Strategie über das Operating Model, die Organisation bis hin zu Prozessverbesserungen und IT-Implementierung), ich bin aber sicher, dass vor allem das Thema Strategie weiterhin ein Feld für die Marktführer bleiben wird."
- „Die großen Prüfungs- und Beratungsfirmen mögen in das Terrain der großen Strategieberater vorzudringen versuchen und auch die IT-Beratungen schielen darauf. Dennoch ticken die Mitarbeiter dieser unterschiedlichen Beratungsanbieter völlig unterschiedlich. In der Praxis werden die Kunden große Unterschiede im Leistungsportfolio ausmachen können, die Frage ist nur, ob man von außen die Unterschiede ausreichend fundiert differenzieren können wird. Das ist eine kommunikative Herausforderung. Wie gut schaffen es die einzelnen Häuser ihren Unique Selling Point in Worte zu fassen? Wer nicht über Kunden sprechen will, tut sich da verdammt schwer. Und so wird es kommunikativ möglicherweise den Anschein machen, dass alle irgendwie das Gleiche anbieten. Daran ändert aber nichts, dass der Trend zum Spezialistentum ungebrochen weitergehen wird und die Qualität am Ende stimmen muss."
- „Auch wenn die Wirtschaftsprüfer vermehrt Strategieberater übernehmen, steht der Beweis [aus], dass der Clash of Cultures zwischen Prüfern und Beratern tatsächlich überwunden werden kann. Bisher haben die Prüfer nur kleinere Beratungshäuser übernommen, spannend wird es, wenn irgendwann mal die Integration eines mittleren oder großen Strategieberaters anstehen sollte."

- „Die Top-Management-Strategieberatung hat ein Wachstums- und Imageproblem nach den rasant verlaufenen 3 vergangenen Jahrzehnten. Eine Ausdifferenzierung findet auf der Relationship-Ebene statt.
  IT-orientierte Beratungen haben Strategie schon seit langem „verschenkt" als ‚loss leader' – aber nicht die erforderliche Glaubwürdigkeit gewonnen.
  Deloitte bleibt da stecken. Accenture auch.
  PWC könnte es schaffen – aber man muss auch wissen dass die EU-Regulierung zu einem großen Umbruch führen wird bei den WP's (massive Wechsel erforderlich, Marktanteile werden sich dramatisch verschieben – was wiederum Auswirkungen auf die Beratung haben wird). KPMG Consulting ist spät dran, E&Y ebenfalls. Und außer Roland Berger will keiner der großen Strategie-Freelancer mehr verkaufen (Verkaufsgründe sind entweder Finanznot oder viele Anteile auf wenige Schultern verteilt)…"
- „Wenngleich es Überlappungen und Interdependenzen gibt, wird es immer einen Markt (d. h. Nachfrage und auch Angebot) für Spezialisten geben."
- „Der Preisdruck wird weiter eine Differenzierung von Tagessätzen erfordern. Das wird wiederum zur Differenzierung von Beratungsfeldern führen und vice versa."

4.4 Bewertung

Tendenziell zeigen sich die Studienteilnehmer der These gegenüber ablehnend. Obwohl die Bemühungen von großen Prüfungs- und IT-Beratungsunternehmen gesehen werden, auf das Feld der Strategieberatung vorstoßen zu wollen, so werden doch Bedenken geäußert, ob in einem solchen Fall z. B. unterschiedliche Unternehmenskulturen harmonisiert werden können. Auch wird angeführt, dass der im Wettbewerb herrschende Preisdruck eine Differenzierung von Tagessätzen und damit von Geschäftsmodellen unterstützt.

Automatisierung von Beratungsleistungen

5

5.1 Einführung

Ein großer Teil der physischen Arbeit ist in den letzten circa 200 Jahren automatisiert worden und die Entwicklungen in der Miniaturisierung und Computerisierung lässt darauf schließen, dass sich diese Entwicklung fortsetzt. Neuartiger sind hingegen die Überlegungen und Arbeiten zur Automatisierung von Wissensarbeit und Managementtätigkeiten.

Managementberatungen helfen ihren Kunden im Umgang mit diesen neuen Technologien und der Automatisierung. Die Selbstreflexion scheint allerdings nur schwach ausgeprägt zu sein. Es sind zwar ausgewählte Pilotaktivitäten zu beobachten und erste wissenschaftliche Beiträge behandeln die (mögliche) Automatisierung von Beratungsleistungen, eine signifikante praktische Umsetzung fehlt allerdings, ebenso wie Business Cases und Volumen- bzw. Marktabschätzungen. Die Frage, wie stark und ob sich Automatisierung auch auf Managementberatung auswirkt, kann also gestellt werden.

5.2 These 2 („Automatisierung")

Managementberatungsleistungen werden innerhalb der nächsten zwei Dekaden zu einem signifikanten Teil (d. h. >30 %) automatisiert sein.

T. Deelmann, *Managementberatung in Deutschland,* essentials,
DOI 10.1007/978-3-658-08892-7_5

5.3 Ergebnisse

Die einzelnen Teilnehmer haben wie folgt Punkte von 5 („Der These stimme ich absolut zu!") bis 1 („Der These stimme ich überhaupt nicht zu!") vergeben:

4, 2, 5, 3, 3, 3, 3, 4, 2, 2, 1, 2, 3, 2. Das arithmetische Mittel beträgt *2,8*. Abbildung 5.1 stellt die Antworten nochmal grafisch dar.

Die Teilnehmer haben zusätzlich folgende *eher zustimmende Kommentare* abgegeben:

- „Plausibel. Vgl. McK-Technologies."
- „Das Internet macht schon heute viele Beratungseinsätze obsolet. Wenn in zwei Jahrzehnten ein Berater engagiert wird, wird man in ihm immer noch den Berater sehen. Aber viele Leistungen, für die heute Berater eingekauft werden, werden dann längst von Maschinen erledigt werden. Die Meinungsbildung und Informationsbeschaffung ist durch das Internet massiv beschleunigt worden. Das wird erst einmal so weitergehen und sich auf immer mehr Felder in tieferem Maße ausdehnen."
- „Halte ich in dem genannten Ausmaß für realistisch, denn ein Großteil der Beraterarbeit besteht aus Benchmarking. Die Grenze ist da erreicht, wo Benchmarking allein nicht mehr reicht und kreative Denkanstöße für ganz neue Geschäftsmodelle notwendig sind."
- „Der Markt, gerade in D[eutschland], ist oftmals aufgebläht – und wird von Digital-Agenturen genau in den Bereichen bedroht, wo Automatisierung möglich und sinnvoll ist. An den „Rändern" stimmt die Hypothese also. […]"

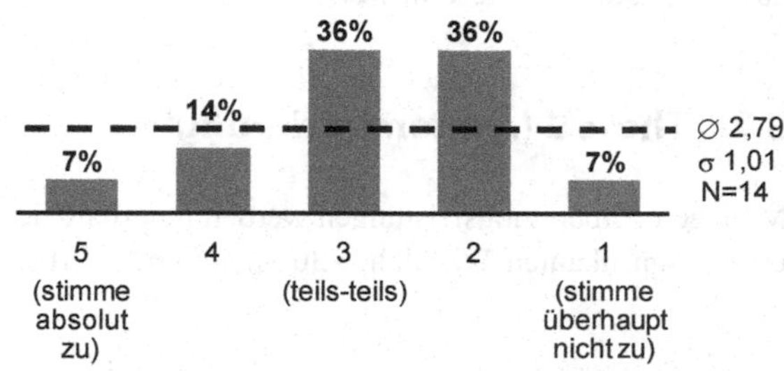

Abb. 5.1 Ergebnisdarstellung zur These der Automatisierung

Die Teilnehmer haben zusätzlich folgende *eher ablehnende Kommentare* abgegeben:

- „[…] Andererseits legen Klienten nach wie vor Wert auf maßgeschneiderte Konzepte und Ansätze – Automatisierung „within" eines Auftrages durchaus möglich (= Kostenabsenkung aufgrund Preisdrucks, z. B. bei Primärresearch übers Internet), nur sehr wenig aber im Verhältnis Klient-Freelancer."
- „Viele Themen rund um Analytik und auch einfache Produktionsschritte wie Graphikerstellung dürften stärker automatisiert werden. Strategieentwicklung, vor allem aber der Beratungsprozess per se, die Auseinandersetzung der Organisation mit den entsprechenden Themen, wird weiter nur in der Zusammenarbeit zwischen Klienten und Berater möglich sein."
- „30 % ist viel. Bin da für die IT-Beratung optimistischer."
- „Die These erscheint mir etwas gewagt: Natürlich gibt es standardisierte Beratungsfelder, wie in der Wirtschaftsprüfung, der Steuerberatung, der Organisations- und Prozessberatung. Aber letztlich sind die Beratungsprobleme so divers wie das Leben. Eine Planung und Automatisierung wird es daher nur in stark datenbasierten Bereichen geben. Dazu gehören auch Befragungen, sowie standardisierte Datenerhebungen."
- „Berater sind innovativ und werden weitere Felder erschließen, auch margenschwächere."
- „Kommt drauf an, was mit Managementberatungsleistungen gemeint ist. Die „Leistung" wird sich womöglich verschieben. Das heißt, wofür bisher bezahlt wurde (hübsche Charts, Prozesstools, Analysen) wird mehr und mehr automatisiert ablaufen können und damit commoditysiert; die eigentliche Beratungsleistung wird sich daher auf schöpferische Geistesleistungen oder soft-skill-affine Dienstleistungen verschieben."
- „Gerade Managementberatung basiert auf Vertrauen."

5.4 Bewertung

Der Automatisierungsthese standen die Experten im Durchschnitt neutral bis leicht ablehnend gegenüber. Der Durchschnittswert von 2,8 täuscht jedoch über die inhaltliche Heterogenität der Befragungsergebnisse hinweg.

So wurde einerseits darauf hingewiesen, dass Beratung primär durch den menschlichen Mitarbeiter geprägt wird, man mithin von einem ‚people business' sprechen kann. Ein solches Geschäft basiert auf Vertrauen und Kreativität ist ein wesentliches Element. Auf der anderen Seite werden die Augen vor dem sich abzeichnenden Automatisierungstrend nicht verschlossen und erste Ansatzpunkte identifiziert. Bei der Analyse sowie der Ergebnisdarstellung könnten sich ausweislich der Einlassungen der Teilnehmer Automatisierungspotenziale einstellen.

Eine Betrachtung des Antwortverhaltens der einzelnen Gruppen lässt aus dem heterogenen Bild des Gesamtergebnisses deutliche Konturen heraustreten: Die von der Automatisierung persönlich weniger stark betroffenen Marktbeobachter stimmen der These deutlich zu. Die aktiv betroffenen Berater lehnen die These hingegen sichtbar ab. Die Gruppe der Kunden liegt zwischen den beiden Extrempositionen.

Auf die ablehnende Haltung der Gruppe der Berater soll kurz eingegangen werden, da sie bemerkenswert erscheint. Mindestens zwei Ansatzpunkte für eine Erklärung sind hier zu sehen: Erstens können Berater über eine Informations- oder Wissensasymmetrie mit Blick auf ihr aktuelles und zukünftige Geschäftsmodell, ihre inneren Strukturen etc. verfügen. Auf Basis dieses Wissens können sie Aussagen mit höherer Präzision zur vorgelegten These tätigen, welche superior zu derjenigen der übrigen beiden Gruppen sind. Zweitens könnte eine ablehnende Position aus einer Haltung des Ausblendens der zu erwartenden negativen Konsequenzen, i. e. die Menge der benötigten Berater und ihre Karrierepfade in den zumeist wachstumsorientierten Beratungen, resultieren. Beide Erklärungspunkte können gemeinsam wirken; weitere Punkte sind ebenfalls denkbar.

6 Reifegrad der Beratungsindustrie

6.1 Einführung

Arthur D. Little bezeichnet sich selbst als die erste und älteste Managementberatung der Welt. Seit der Gründung im Jahr 1886 sind fast 130 Jahre vergangen und verschiedentlich wird postuliert, dass es sich bei der Beratungsbranche um eine „reife“ Branche handelt.

Gleichzeitig ist die Anbieterstruktur sehr kleinteilig und Konzentrationsgrade sind gering.

Es drängt sich vor diesem Hintergrund die Frage auf, ob die Beratungsbranche tatsächlich saturiert ist.

6.2 These 3 („Reife")

Die Managementberatung kann als „reife“ Branche bezeichnet werden.

6.3 Ergebnisse

Die einzelnen Teilnehmer haben wie folgt Punkte von 5 („Der These stimme ich absolut zu!“) bis 1 („Der These stimme ich überhaupt nicht zu!“) vergeben:

3, 4, 5, 5, 2, 5, 4, 4, 4, 4, 4, 3, 5, 4. Das arithmetische Mittel beträgt *4,0*. Abbildung 6.1 stellt die Antworten nochmal grafisch dar.

T. Deelmann, *Managementberatung in Deutschland,* essentials,
DOI 10.1007/978-3-658-08892-7_6

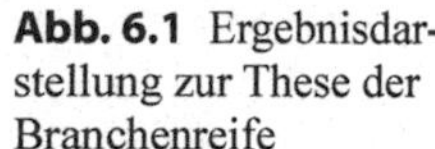

Abb. 6.1 Ergebnisdarstellung zur These der Branchenreife

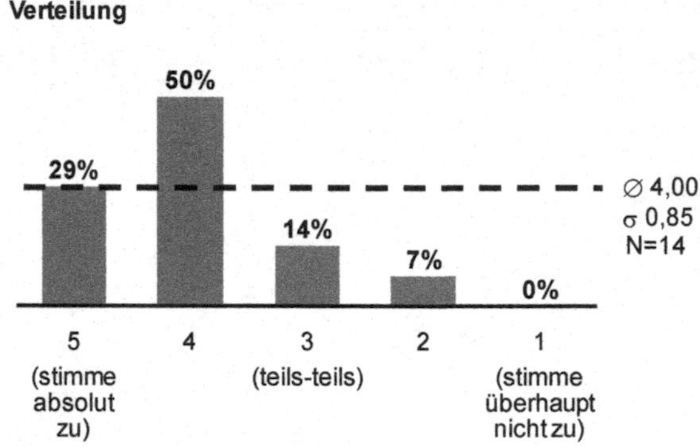

Die Teilnehmer haben zusätzlich folgende *eher zustimmende Kommentare* abgegeben:

- „Ja – Der Markt wächst nur noch langsam, der Wettbewerb ist intensive und oligopolistisch, das Einkaufsverhalten der Klienten ist transaktional und die Preise sind transparent…"
- „Die Branche ist aus meiner Sicht schon allein deshalb als reif zu bezeichnen, weil es einfach schon viele Alumni gibt."
- „Die Konsolidierung des Marktes, das End-Game, zeigt eine starke Konsolidierung des Marktes. Legt man das Markt-Spektrum auf so genannte Gesamtmärkte (Europa, Asien) dann stimmt diese These. Es gibt aber noch eine Reihe von Märkten, wo die Beratung noch nicht zur Reife gekommen ist."
- „Reif in dem Sinne, dass sich die Leistungen ausdifferenzieren, ein Konzentrationsprozess läuft und die Profitabilität sinkt."
- „Reif im Sinne: Methoden sind ausgereift, in großen Teilen ist verdrängungsartiger Wettbewerb um Marktanteile in Teil- bzw. Nischenmärkten."
- „[Beratung] hat mehrere Zyklen durchlaufen, die für „reife" Branchen typisierend sind."

Die Teilnehmer haben zusätzlich folgende *eher ablehnende Kommentare* abgegeben:

- „Reif ist was anderes, aber die Branche ändert sich."
- „Reife einer Branche kann man an unterschiedlichen Faktoren festmachen. Generell stehen manche Entwicklungen der „Industrialisierung" den Dienstleistungen noch bevor. Nicht alle Ideen aus dem Sachgüterbereich lassen sich aber

auf DL [vermutlich gemeint: Dienstleistungen, d. Verf.] in gleichem Umfang übertragen.“

- „Starke Ausdifferenzierung in Fachberatungen (z. B. Supply Chain, Sourcing, IT, Restrukturierung etc.) hat stattgefunden; dennoch wäre eine reife Industrie erst da, wenn ein relativ hoher Konsolidierungsgrad vorliegt – das ist nicht der Fall.“
- „Die Mechanismen haben sich viele Jahre nicht geändert. Lediglich neue Inhalte werden mit bekannten Tools verkauft.“

6.4 Bewertung

Die These über die Branchenreife hat einen sehr hohen Zustimmungswert von den Teilnehmern erhalten.

Die Kommentare erwähnen beispielsweise ausdifferenzierte Leistungen, ausgereifte Methoden und ein verlangsamtes Marktwachstum zur Unterstützung der These.

In einer Rückmeldung wird jedoch darauf hingewiesen, dass eine Industrie formal als ‚reif‘ bezeichnet werden kann, wenn eine hohe Anbieterkonzentration vorliegt – was in der Beratung nicht der Fall ist: So kommen die drei größten Managementberatungen in 2011 auf einen kumulierten Marktanteil von circa 11 % und die zehn größten Managementberatungen auf ca. 24 %.

Die ‚tatsächliche‘ Reife scheint also von der ‚gefühlten‘ abzuweichen.

7 Relevanz des deutschen Beratungsmarktes im internationalen Kontext

7.1 Einführung

Der deutsche Beratungsmarkt scheint eine gewisse Relevanz für internationale Beratungsunternehmen aufzuweisen. Neben der relativ und absolut hohen Zahl von Büros (vgl. für Details auch weiter unten) scheint auch die Anzahl der mit Deutschen besetzten internationalen Führungspositionen in Beratungsunternehmen überdurchschnittlich hoch zu sein.

Es stellt sich die Frage, ob diese Relevanz vor dem Hintergrund neuer Wachstumsmärkte beibehalten werden kann oder ob sie tendenziell abnimmt.

Als Proxy für die Relevanz des deutschen Beratungsmarktes könnte die Anzahl der deutschen Büros großer Strategieberatungen (A.T. Kearney, Bain & Company, The Boston Consulting Group, McKinsey & Company und Roland Berger Strategy Consultants) und damit die Bindung finanzieller Mittel, die nicht in andere Märkte investiert werden können, herangezogen werden.

7.2 These 4 („Relevanz")

Die Relevanz des deutschen Beratungsmarktes nimmt bis 2019 im internationalen Vergleich merklich ab. (Dies kann ausgedrückt werden durch die Anzahl der Büros, von denen statt heute 28 nur noch 20 oder weniger vorhanden sein werden.)

T. Deelmann, *Managementberatung in Deutschland,* essentials,
DOI 10.1007/978-3-658-08892-7_7

7.3 Ergebnisse

Die einzelnen Teilnehmer haben wie folgt Punkte von 5 („Der These stimme ich absolut zu!“) bis 1 („Der These stimme ich überhaupt nicht zu!“) vergeben: *2, 4, 3, 3, 4, 2, 4, 4, 3, 1, 4, 1, 3, 4*. Das arithmetische Mittel beträgt *3,0*. Abbildung 7.1 stellt die Antworten nochmal grafisch dar.

Die Teilnehmer haben zusätzlich folgende *eher zustimmende Kommentare* abgegeben:

- „Das stellen wir in unserem Unternehmen fest. Neue Märkte, v. a. in Asien und neuerdings Afrika, spielen eine immer größere Rolle, Revenue-mäßig aber auch bei der Entwicklung neuer Themen.“
- „Der Höhepunkt der Bedeutung des deutschen Beratermarkts ist schon vorbei. Vor zehn Jahren waren viele Weltchefs Deutsche. Die Bedeutung wird weiter abnehmen, wobei der typisch deutsche Beratungsstil sicher international angesehen ist – hohes Spezialistenwissen, Ingenieurstugenden, gewisse Profundität der Beratungsleistung.“
- „Die Welt schaut nach Asien.“
- „Das erschiene mir nur logisch, denn letztlich folgt das Beratungsgeschäft den Globalisierungstrends. Schon heute erzielen die Beratungsunternehmen in China höhere Wachstumsraten als in den beiden (noch) umsatzstärksten Märkten USA und Deutschland. Wenn der Trend anhält – und davon ist auszugehen – wird das [gemeint sind hier vermutlich die Wachstumsraten, d. Verf.] so bleiben.“
- „Die Frage ist, ob Büros ein guter Indikator ist. Es wird grundsätzlich viel weniger Büros für jede Art von Tätigkeit geben, Beratungen werden eine gewisse

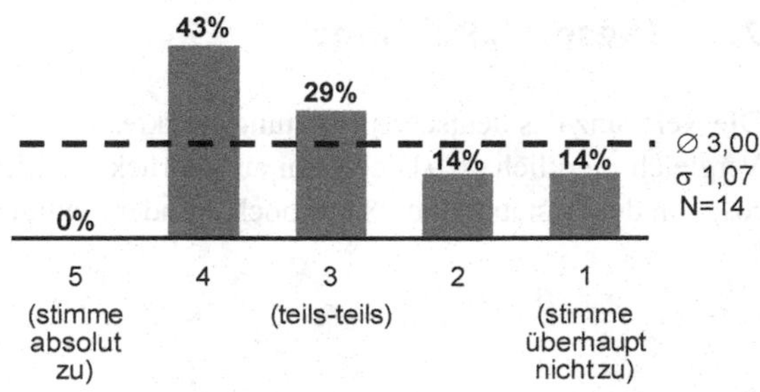

Abb. 7.1 Ergebnisdarstellung zur These der Rolle im internationalen Vergleich

Vorreiterrolle haben. Das Marktvolumen wird jedenfalls nicht schrumpfen – nur relativ, weil andere wachsen."
- „Die Bedeutung nimmt linear mit der Bedeutung der deutschen Industrie im internationalen Kontext ab."

Die Teilnehmer haben zusätzlich folgende *eher ablehnende Kommentare* abgegeben:

- „Schon durch das Wachstum in Asien, Südamerika und Afrika [nimmt die Relevanz des deutschen Marktes ab, d. Verf.], aber nicht darüber hinaus. Deutschland ist m. E. für die Beratung so wichtig, weil die Kultur Beratung begünstigt. Deutsche überlegen [sic! Vermutlich und mit Blick auf den nächsten Satz ist ‚überleben' gemeint, d. Verf.] nur bei enger Steuerung, können nicht improvisieren wie z. B. die Brasilianer, oder verkaufen wie Amerikaner und sind nicht so unternehmerisch wie die Chinesen. Sie überleben durch Fachwissen und Steuerung. Z. B. ist Deutschland in Sachen ERP führend, wegen der starken akademischen Tradition, die auch SAP begünstigt hat. Die Formalisierung und Versachlichung der Führung ist Teil der Beratung und wird in Deutschland stärker betrieben als woanders."
- „Ich würde der These weniger zustimmen, da ich glaube, dass deutsche Beratungen in den nächsten Jahren eher international expandieren werden."
- „Ich sehe keine besondere Relevanz. Vielmehr halte ich die Qualifikation von deutschen Beratern für höher, so dass sie auf mehr Nachfrage stoßen."
- „Deutschland wird seine Rolle als ‚lead market' in Europe behalten und noch ausbauen. Erst nach 2018 bin ich da skeptischer, wenn man die Langzeitauswirkungen der aktuellen deutschen Politik betrachtet, die zu einer klaren Schwächung der deutschen Wettbewerbsfähigkeit führen wird."
- „Unsicher, weil deutsche Beratungsleistungen im Ausland durchaus eine steigende Nachfrage erwarten können, jedoch innerhalb Deutschlands eine gewisse Professionalisierung innerhalb der Klientel der Managementberater dazu führen kann, dass weniger externe Beratung nachgefragt wird. International herrscht im Vergleich sicher etwas „Nachholbedarf"."

7.4 Bewertung

Die Teilnehmer stehen der These im Durchschnitt ambivalent gegenüber. In der Einzelbetrachtung der Kommentare lassen sich jedoch zwei unterschiedliche Lager identifizieren:

Auf der einen Seite wird die vorhandene Kultur, Arbeitseinstellung und Qualität der Berater in Deutschland herausgestellt und sogar ein Ausbau der Position durch Expansionen erwartet.

Auf der anderen Seite wird mehrfach das Marktwachstum in Asien (und perspektivisch Afrika) genannt – und in einem Kommentar werden auch neue regionale Schwerpunkte bei der sog. Themenentwicklung gesehen.

8 Explizit artikulierte und nicht explizit artikulierte Beratungsbedarfe

8.1 Einführung

Typische und regelmäßig vorgebrachte Beratungsbedarfe bestehen z. B. in einer nicht vorhandenen Expertise oder in mangelnden Ressourcen. Der Wunsch nach Befriedigung dieser Bedarfe wird zumeist explizit artikuliert.

In der Praxis sind zudem Fälle beobachtbar, in denen beispielsweise ein Sündenbock, ein Guru oder ein Legitimator gesucht werden und der Berater diese Rolle übernimmt. Oftmals wird jedoch nicht dieser tatsächliche Bedarf in den Vordergrund gestellt, sondern nur in Form einer „hidden agenda" verfolgt; er ist also nicht explizit artikuliert.

Berater, die solche nicht explizit artikulierten Bedarfe befriedigen (sollen), laufen Gefahr, Konflikte zu produzieren, wenn sie nicht über die Rollenerwartung informiert sind, da der erwartete und der bearbeitete Projektinhalt variieren kann. Eine größere Transparenz über den konkreten Beauftragungsgrund würde das Konfliktpotential verringern. Die Domäne der Klientenprofessionalisierung kann an dieser Stelle unterstützen.

8.2 These 5 („Bedarfe")

Heute in der Managementberatung nicht explizit artikulierte Beratungsbedarfe (z. B. nach einem Legitimator oder Guru) werden im Jahr 2019 deutlich häufiger explizit beauftragt und einen sichtbaren Anteil (d. h. >10 %) aller Beauftragungen ausmachen.

T. Deelmann, *Managementberatung in Deutschland,* essentials,
DOI 10.1007/978-3-658-08892-7_8

8.3 Ergebnisse

Die einzelnen Teilnehmer haben wie folgt Punkte von 5 („Der These stimme ich absolut zu!“) bis 1 („Der These stimme ich überhaupt nicht zu!“) vergeben:

3, 5, 1, 2, 1, 5, 1, 3, 1, 1, 5, 3, 2, 3. Das arithmetische Mittel beträgt *2,6.* Abbildung 8.1 stellt die Antworten nochmal grafisch dar.

Die Teilnehmer haben zusätzlich folgende *eher zustimmende Kommentare* abgegeben:

- „Diese Entwicklung ist heute bereits abzusehen – sehr spezifische, enge Bedarfe nach herausragender Expertise oder nach Coaching/ Team-Begleitung werden immer wichtiger.“
- „Ich gehe von einer weiteren Professionalisierung der Klienten aus, so dass Einsätze, die nicht streng professionell oder sachlich begründet sind, eher abnehmen.“
- „Heute sind in faktisch allen Managementberatungsprojekten zumindest Teile einer Hidden Agenda versteckt.“

Die Teilnehmer haben zusätzlich folgende *eher ablehnende Kommentare* abgegeben:

- „Der Anteil könnte wegen [einer] Klientenprofessionalisierung allenfalls abnehmen. Ich glaube aber, nicht signifikant.“
- „Kann keinen Änderungsgrund erkennen.“
- „Wünschenswert wäre das auf jeden Fall – aber wer hätte ein Interesse daran? Die nach einem Legitimator suchenden Top-Manager sicher nicht, die Berater

Abb. 8.1 Ergebnisdarstellung zur These der Bedarfsartikulation

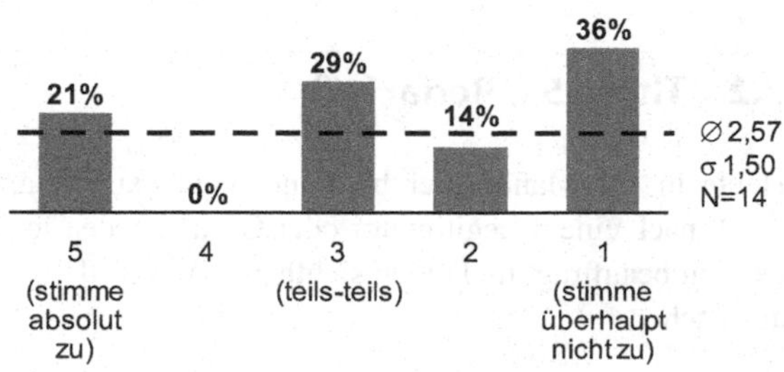

aber auch nicht, denn bei denen geht es ums Geschäft. Getrieben werden könnte eine solche Entwicklung aber zum Beispiel von den Aufsichtsräten oder den Stakeholdern eines Unternehmens, nämlich wenn die von den Vorständen Begründungen für die Vergabe von Beratungsaufträgen verlangen."

- „Ich glaube nicht, dass sich dies im Gegensatz zu heute großartig verändert. Auch heute gibt es im Markt Leuchtturme und Gurus, für die überdurchschnittliche Tagessätze bezahlt werden."
- „Wenn das nicht ein Hinweis auf Reife ist ...:-)"
- „[...] Es gibt den latenten Bedarf heute und wird ihn auch in Zukunft geben. Aber er wird nie wirklich so beauftragt werden, sondern zumeist unter einem fachlichen Vorwand – keiner will seinen Job verlieren, und jeder muss [sich] rechtfertigen, warum er einen Freelancer unter Vertrag nimmt..."
- „Dies würde den Grund für den impliziten Auftrag vernichten und damit den Auftrag ad absurdum führen."

8.4 Bewertung

Dem arithmetischen Mittel von 2,6 folgend, wird die These neutral bis leicht ablehnend betrachtet. Hinzuweisen ist jedoch auf die Spreizung der Antworten. Eine kleine Gruppe stimmt der Aussage absolut zu, während eine etwas größere Gruppe eine ablehnende Position vertritt.

Die Analyse der einzelnen Teilnehmergruppen zeigt, dass bei den Beratern und den Kunden Extrempositionen vertreten sind, dass es also Teilnehmer gibt, die fest davon ausgehen, dass es zu einer neuen Ehrlichkeit und Offenheit in der Zusammenarbeit kommen wird und muss, und dass es welche gibt, die der Meinung sind, dass ebendieses nicht eintritt. Die Marktbeobachter zeigen sich neutral bis ablehnend.

Die Gemengelage scheint hier sehr dichotom zu sein. Die Kommentare weisen z. B. einerseits darauf hin, dass eine zunehmende Klientenprofessionalisierung die nicht explizit artikulierten Bedarfe eher abnehmen lässt; andererseits aber auch, dass die Explizierung bereits heute in der Auftragslage sichtbar ist.

Ob es tatsächlich zu einer Veränderung kommt, erscheint fraglich. Ein signifikanter Impuls fehlt und Anbieter und Nachfrager haben sich in diesem Graubereich der gegenseitigen Ehrlichkeit eingerichtet. Ihr Interesse an einer Veränderung dieser Situation scheint nicht sehr ausgeprägt.

9 Office-Dichte der großen Strategieberatungen in Deutschland

9.1 Einführung

Deutschland verfügt nach den USA über die größte absolute Anzahl von Büros der internationalen Management- bzw. Strategieberatungen A.T. Kearney, Bain & Company, The Boston Consulting Group, McKinsey & Company und Roland Berger Strategy Consultants.

Auch wenn die Anzahl der Büros in Relation zum Bruttoinlandsprodukt oder zur Bevölkerungsmenge gesetzt wird, nimmt Deutschland im relativen Vergleich zu anderen G20-Staaten eine Spitzenposition ein.

Es kann also die Frage gestellt werden, warum die Anzahl und Dichte der Büros in Deutschland so hoch ist? Nachfolgend werden sechs Thesen als mögliche Antworten diskutiert.

9.2 These 6.1 („Auf den Grund gehen")

Unternehmen in Deutschland gehen Sachverhalten und Problemen gerne „auf den Grund" und fragen deshalb relativ viel Beratungsleistungen nach, was sich indirekt in der Anzahl der Büros niederschlägt.

T. Deelmann, *Managementberatung in Deutschland,* essentials,
DOI 10.1007/978-3-658-08892-7_9

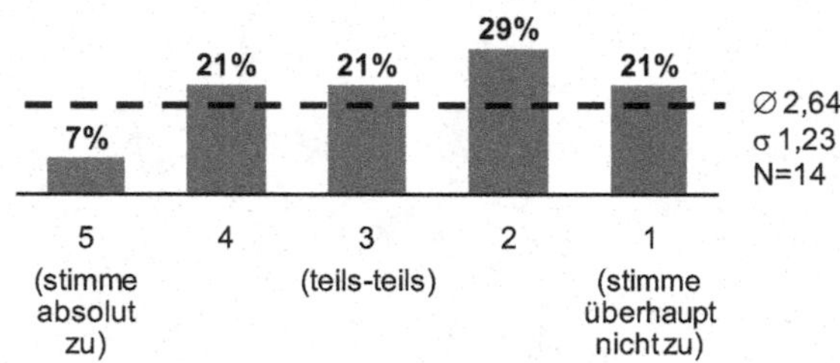

Abb. 9.1 Ergebnisdarstellung zur These der Gründlichkeit. (Differenz der Einzelwerte zu 100 % auf Grund von Rundungen)

9.3 Ergebnisse

Die einzelnen Teilnehmer haben wie folgt Punkte von 5 („Der These stimme ich absolut zu!") bis 1 („Der These stimme ich überhaupt nicht zu!") vergeben:

5, 2, 1, 3, 4, 2, 1, 2, 1, 3, 4, 4, 2, 3. Das arithmetische Mittel beträgt *2,6*. Abbildung 9.1 stellt die Antworten nochmal grafisch dar.

Die Teilnehmer haben zusätzlich folgende *eher ablehnende Kommentare* abgegeben:

- „Das halte ich nicht für einen Treiber."
- „Ein signifikanter Anteil der deutschen Beraterkapazitäten ist im Ausland tätig. Dies kann nicht zum deutschen Markt gezählt werden. Dass so viele im Ausland sind, liegt an der zentralen geografischen Lage und insbesondere an der besseren Qualifikation der deutschen Berater. Die Bevorzugung deutscher Berater reicht sogar bis in die USA."
- „Mag sein, dass man in Deutschland gerne „auf den Grund geht" – dies ist jedoch nicht ursächlich für die Anzahl der Büros. (Korrelation ist nicht gleich Kausalität.)"

9.4 Bewertung

Die Teilnehmer verteilen ihre Einschätzungen gegenüber der These fast gleichmäßig über alle Antwortmöglichkeiten.

Im Durchschnitt wird sie jedoch schwach abgelehnt und scheint daher nicht geeignet, die hohe Anzahl der vorhandenen Büros (Niederlassungen) der großen Strategieberater in Deutschland zu erklären.

9.5 These 6.2 („Managementstil")

Unternehmen in Deutschland verfolgen traditionell einen Managementstil, der im internationalen Vergleich eher auf Kooperation (und weniger auf Wettbewerb, wie z. B. in den USA) ausgelegt ist und zudem die Unternehmensführung relativ oft in der Hand von angestellten Managern liegt (und weniger oft in den Händen der Eigentümer, wie z. B. in England), so dass diese Vorprägung die Nachfrage nach Beratungsleistungen und auch die Anzahl der Büros begünstigt.

9.6 Ergebnisse

Die einzelnen Teilnehmer haben wie folgt Punkte von 5 („Der These stimme ich absolut zu!") bis 1 („Der These stimme ich überhaupt nicht zu!") vergeben:

5, 2, 1, 4, 2, 2, 3, 4, 1, 3, 4, 2, 5, 4. Das arithmetische Mittel beträgt *3,0*. Abbildung 9.2 stellt die Antworten nochmal grafisch dar.

Die Teilnehmer haben zusätzlich folgenden *eher zustimmenden Kommentar* abgegeben:

- „Plausibel und außerdem deckungsgleich mit meiner Erfahrung, dass deutsche Manager sich gerne „absichern" wollen und man sich generell gerne Autoritäten fügt (im internationalen Vergleich). (Warum jedoch eine Wettbewerbsorientierung weniger Nachfrage nach Beratungsleistungen erzeugt, ist mir nicht schlüssig [Dieser Schluss war auch im Rahmen der These so nicht intendiert, d. Verf.] – auch das Gegenteil könnte der Fall sein.)"

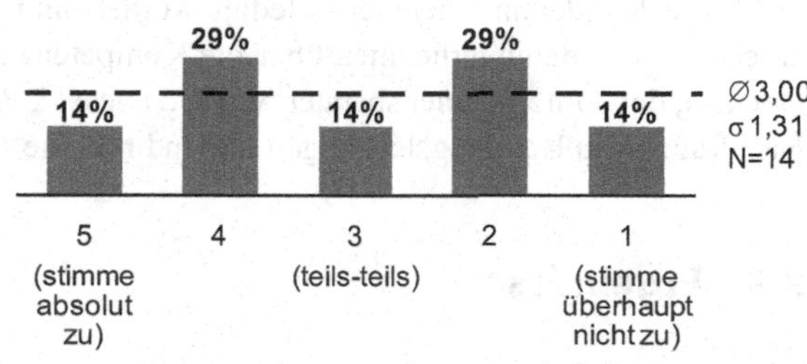

Abb. 9.2 Ergebnisdarstellung zur These des Managementstils

Die Teilnehmer haben zusätzlich folgenden *eher ablehnenden Kommentar* abgegeben:

- „M.E. auch nicht so relevant."

9.7 Bewertung

Der in dieser These enthaltene Erklärungsversuch vermag die Teilnehmer nicht vollständig zu überzeugen.

Allerdings ist eine sehr große Spreizung der Einschätzungen zu beobachten.

9.8 These 6.3 („Rollentausch")

Unter anderem das in einigen Managementberatungen vorherrschende „Up or Out"-Prinzip, aber auch die individuelle Lebensplanung einzelner Berater hat dazu geführt, dass die ehemaligen Berater mit ihrem dort erworbenen Wissen in Kundenunternehmen arbeiten. Hierdurch wird die Wissensasymmetrie zwischen Beratung und Kunde, also das herkömmliche Vertriebsargument der Beratung, c. p. unwichtiger.

Parallel ist zu beobachten, dass viele Kundenunternehmen eine personelle Verschlankung vorgenommen haben, ohne jedoch die Ablauforganisation entsprechend anzupassen. Die herkömmlichen Geschäftsprozesse müssen nun mit einer kleineren Menge an Personal durchgeführt werden. Dies gelingt nicht in allen Fällen, so dass für (ehemalige) Regeltätigkeiten temporäre Unterstützung von Dritten benötigt wird.

Es kann die folgende These formuliert werden: Es hat sich eine Art „Rollentausch" vollzogen, bei dem Berater teilweise die Aufgaben übernehmen, die früher durch die Kundenunternehmen erledigt wurden und bei dem ausgewählte Mitarbeiter in Kundenunternehmen über die Kompetenzen verfügen, die früher eine Domäne der Unternehmensberater waren. Dieser „Rollentausch" befördert die Nachfrage nach Beratungsleistungen und indirekt die Anzahl der Büros.

9.9 Ergebnisse

Die einzelnen Teilnehmer haben wie folgt Punkte von 5 („Der These stimme ich absolut zu!") bis 1 („Der These stimme ich überhaupt nicht zu!") vergeben:

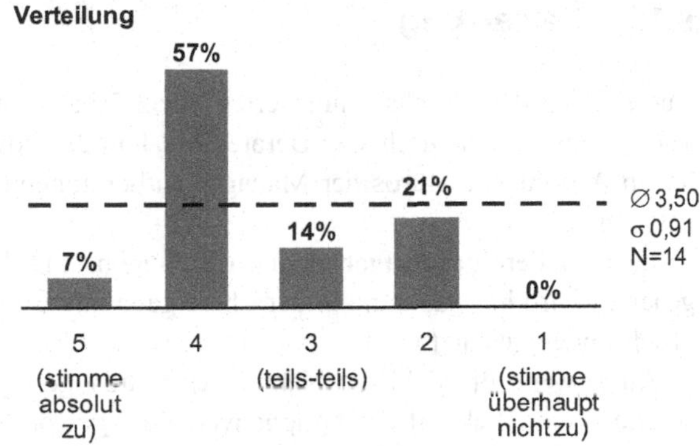

Abb. 9.3 Ergebnisdarstellung zur These des Rollentausches. (Differenz der Einzelwerte zu 100 % auf Grund von Rundungen)

2, 2, 3, 4, 4, 4, 5, 2, 4, 4, 4, 3, 4, 4. Das arithmetische Mittel beträgt *3,5*. Abbildung 9.3 stellt die Antworten nochmal grafisch dar.

Die Teilnehmer haben zusätzlich folgende *eher zustimmende Kommentare* abgegeben:

- „Sicherlich [liegt] das auch an der sehr dezentralen Struktur in Deutschland. Sonst hätten große Beratungen nicht in Düsseldorf und Köln Büros."
- „Ist nachweislich der Fall. Oft ‚verkommt' die externe Dienstleistung zur Prozessberatung. Wenn dies in signifikant vielen Fällen geschieht, wird es zum Standardmodell und befördert damit am Ende die Zahl der Büros."

Die Teilnehmer haben zusätzlich folgende *eher ablehnende Kommentare* abgegeben:

- „Der Rollentausch befördert ja nicht die Nachfrage, sondern ändert eher ihre Zusammensetzung, und zwar verlagert sie [sich] tendenziell [in] Richtung niedrigerer Wertschöpfung."
- „M.E. auch nicht so relevant."
- „Der Rollenwechsel – Berater wird Vorstand eines ehemaligen Kunden – müsste eigentlich eher dazu führen, dass die Nachfrage nach Beratungsleistungen abnimmt, weil das Know-how ja ins Unternehmen gewechselt ist."
- „Das ist zwar einen richtige Grundbeobachtung, hat aber mit der Bürodichte in D[eutschland] nichts zu tun."

9.10 Bewertung

Ausweislich des Durchschnittswertes von 3,5 haben die befragten Experten der These zum Rollentausch von Berater und Kunden sowie zur Ursächlichkeit der hohen Anzahl von Büros der Managementberatungen in Deutschland leicht zugestimmt.

Insbesondere der Aufgabentausch ist Gegenstand der Freitextantworten. Festgehalten wird hier, dass die in der These genannte Entwicklung durch eigene Beobachtungen gestützt wird.

Auch wenn die Zahl der Nennungen relativ gering ist, so soll auch für diese These ein Blick auf das Gruppenverhalten geworfen werden: Die Gruppe der Kunden unterstützt die These am stärksten. Das Gruppenergebnis liegt 0,6 Punkte über dem Ergebnis der Gruppe der Berater und 0,8 Punkte über der Gruppe der Marktbeobachter.

Mit Blick auf die Einlassungen der Teilnehmer hat der sich auf die Bürodichte in Deutschland beziehende Teil der These keinen Zuspruch erhalten. Besser sieht es hingegen mit dem Aufgabentausch aus. Hier teilen die Teilnehmer die Beobachtung, dass Berater oftmals Aufgaben übernehmen, die vor einer Reorganisationen und Arbeitsplatzreduzierungen durch Kundenmitarbeiter ausgeführt haben wurden.

Eine Folgethese könnte also lauten, dass Organisationen zwar die Aufgabe „Personalabbau" erfolgreich angehen, die damit aber einhergehende Aufgabe „Veränderung der Aufbau- und Ablauforganisation" vernachlässigen. Die auftretenden personellen Lücken werden schließlich durch externe Ressourcen, hier: Berater, geschlossen. Dadurch entwickelt sich eine neue Form der organisatorischen Zusammenarbeit und Grenzziehung.

9.11 These 6.4 („Obrigkeits-Bejahung")

In Deutschland wird oftmals der Hang zu einer „Obrigkeits-Bejahung" vermutet. Auch Berater können dieses Bedürfnis befriedigen. Dies wirkt sich positiv auf die Nachfrage nach Beratungsleistungen aus, die sich wiederum indirekt in der Anzahl der Büros niederschlägt.

9.12 Ergebnisse

Die einzelnen Teilnehmer haben wie folgt Punkte von 5 („Der These stimme ich absolut zu!") bis 1 („Der These stimme ich überhaupt nicht zu!") vergeben:

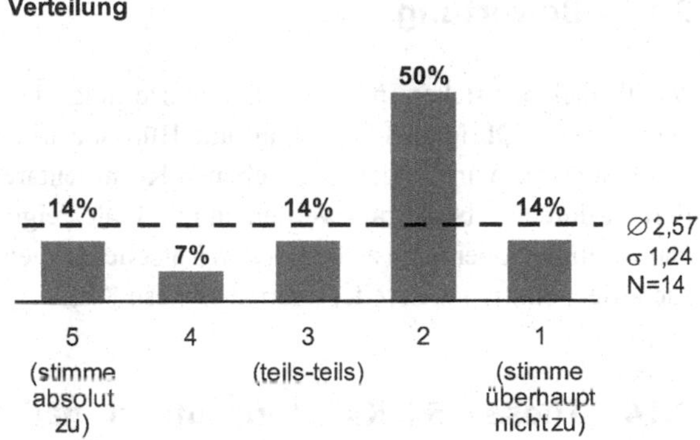

Abb. 9.4 Ergebnisdarstellung zur These der Obrigkeits-Bejahung. (Differenz der Einzelwerte zu 100 % auf Grund von Rundungen)

5, 2, 1, 4, 2, 3, 2, 2, 2, 1, 2, 3, 5, 2. Das arithmetische Mittel beträgt *2,6*. Abbildung 9.4 stellt die Antworten nochmal grafisch dar.

Die Teilnehmer haben zusätzlich folgenden *eher zustimmenden Kommentar* abgegeben:

- „Siehe meinen Kommentar zu 6.2."
  [„Plausibel und außerdem deckungsgleich mit meiner Erfahrung, dass deutsche Manager sich gerne „absichern" wollen und man sich generell gerne Autoritäten fügt (im internationalen Vergleich). (Warum jedoch eine Wettbewerbsorientierung weniger Nachfrage nach Beratungsleistungen erzeugt, ist mir nicht schlüssig [Dieser Schluss war auch im Rahmen der These so nicht intendiert, d. Verf.] – auch das Gegenteil könnte der Fall sein.)"]

Die Teilnehmer haben zusätzlich folgende *eher ablehnende Kommentare* abgegeben:

- „M.E. auch nicht so relevant."
- „Natürlich sind Berater immer auch ein wenig Feigenblatt [bei, d. Verf.] Management-Entscheidungen. Ich glaube aber nicht, dass dies etwas mit Obrigkeitshörigkeit zu tun hat."
- „Ein höchstens sehr indirekter Effekt auf die Bürodichte und die Anzahl der Berater…"

9.13 Bewertung

Die Teilnehmer stehen in der Gesamtbeurteilung dieser These und insb. der Verbindung von ‚Obrigkeits-Bejahung' und Büroanzahl eher ablehnend gegenüber.

Gleichwohl wird in den abgegebenen Kommentaren darauf hingewiesen, dass Berater durchaus beauftragt werden, um z. B. als Feigenblatt bzw. zur Absicherung von getätigten oder noch zu tätigenden Entscheidungen der Kunden zu dienen (vgl. auch die Kommentare weiter oben zur These 8.2).

9.14 These 6.5 („Klientenprofessionalisierung")

Die sog. „Klientenprofessionalisierung" ist in Deutschland noch nicht ausreichend ausgeprägt. Dies macht es Beratungen relativ leicht, Projekte zu verkaufen. Die resultierende relativ hohe Nachfrage nach Beratungsleistungen bedingt wiederum organisatorisch die hohe Anzahl der Büros.

9.15 Ergebnisse

Die einzelnen Teilnehmer haben wie folgt Punkte von 5 („Der These stimme ich absolut zu!") bis 1 („Der These stimme ich überhaupt nicht zu!") vergeben:

2, 1, 1, 2, 4, 3, 1, 2, 2, 2, 1, 2, 5, 1. Das arithmetische Mittel beträgt *2,1*. Abbildung 9.5 stellt die Antworten nochmal grafisch dar.

Die Teilnehmer haben zusätzlich folgenden *eher zustimmenden Kommentar* abgegeben:

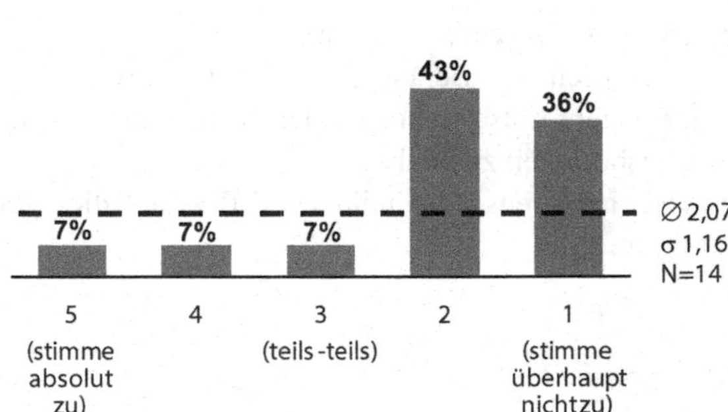

Abb. 9.5 Ergebnisdarstellung zur These der Klientenprofessionalisierung

- „Siehe meinen Kommentar zu These 4 [„Unsicher, weil deutsche Beratungsleistungen im Ausland durchaus eine steigende Nachfrage erwarten können, jedoch innerhalb Deutschlands eine gewisse Professionalisierung innerhalb der Klientel der Managementberater dazu führen kann, dass weniger externe Beratung nachgefragt wird. International herrscht im Vergleich sicher etwas „Nachholbedarf".", d. Verf.] – ist heute wahrscheinlich tatsächlich so, wird sich jedoch perspektivisch und im internationalen Vergleich ändern."

Die Teilnehmer haben zusätzlich folgende *eher ablehnende Kommentare* abgegeben:

- „Es mag sein, dass die Klientenprofessionalisierung in US und EK [vermutlich ist „UK" gemeint, d. Verf.] weiter vorangeschritten ist als in D[eutschland], ansonsten erscheint mir dies nicht so überzeugend."
- „Der deutsche Markt ist deutlich schwieriger als in den USA/UK. Die Klienten sind m. E. deutlich professioneller."
- „Ich denke das die Firmen, die heute Managementberatungsleistungen kaufen in den letzten Jahren eher noch gewachsen ist, weil auch mittelständische Firmen heute Beratung kaufen können."
- „Trotz hoher Nachfrage wird es m. E. mittelfristig weniger Büros (bei den großen Beratungen) geben."

9.16 Bewertung

Die These erhält zwar vereinzelt Zustimmung, das Mittel von 2,07 ist aber der niedrigste Wert im Thema 6 (Office-Dichte).

Interessant allerdings auch hier wieder der Blick auf die einzelnen Teilnehmergruppen: Während Berater und Marktbeobachter die These ablehnen, stehen die Kunden ihr eher positiv gegenüber.

Es könnte also vermutet werden, dass das Eigenbild der Kunden hinsichtlich ihrer Professionalisierung vom Fremdbild abweicht. Hierzu passt auch ein Beraterkommentar, in dem der deutsche Markt im internationalen Vergleich als eher schwierig dargestellt wird.

9.17 These 6.6 („Dezentrale Wirtschaftsstruktur")

In Deutschland findet sich, ggf. getrieben durch den Mittelstand, eine eher „dezentrale Wirtschaftsstruktur" vor. Um diese angemessen bedienen und eine große Kundennähe zeigen zu können, sind entsprechend relativ viele Büros vorhanden.

9.18 Ergebnisse

Die einzelnen Teilnehmer haben wie folgt Punkte von 5 („Der These stimme ich absolut zu!") bis 1 („Der These stimme ich überhaupt nicht zu!") vergeben: *2, 4, 5, 4, 4, 4, 4, 4, 5, 5, 4, 4, 3, 4*. Das arithmetische Mittel beträgt *4,0*. Abbildung 9.6 stellt die Antworten nochmal grafisch dar.

Die Teilnehmer haben zusätzlich folgende *eher zustimmende Kommentare* abgegeben:

- „Die dezentrale Struktur der Wirtschaft ist m. E. der Haupttreiber der vielen Büros – anders als z. B. in UK ist es sinnvoll (und für Mitarbeiter auch attraktiv) an verschiedenen Standorten präsent zu sein. Für uns [gemeint ist hier ein Beratungshaus, d. Verf.] ist der Aspekt „Recruiting" durchaus wichtig – wo wollen Berater leben/arbeiten…"
- „Die Bürodichte ist durch die Dezentralität (viele ähnlich große Ballungsräume erfordern jeweils Büros in der Nähe) Deutschlands bedingt."
- „Das [d. h. diese These im Vergleich] am ehesten. In Wirklichkeit hat es auch mit der Frage zu tun, [ob] die Klienten wegen der dezentralen Wirtschaftsstruktur bereit sind, die Reisekosten zu bezahlen, so dass die Beratungsunterneh-

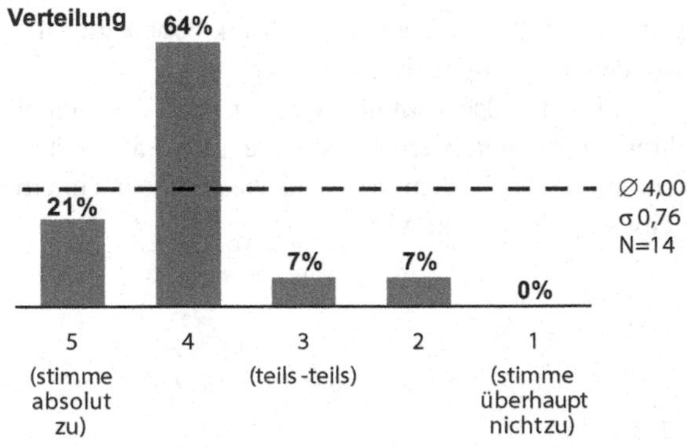

Abb. 9.6 Ergebnisdarstellung zur These der dezentralen Wirtschaftsstruktur. (Differenz der Einzelwerte zu 100 % auf Grund von Rundungen)

men ein Incentive haben, der Sehnsucht der jungen Freelancer nach „ihrem" Wunsch-Wohnort nachzugeben…"

- „Kenne dafür die Zahlen zu wenig (ABC-Analyse der Wirtschaftskraft vs. Anzahl Unternehmen). Aber nur weil es ‚viele kleine' statt ‚wenige große' Kunden gibt, muss dies zu mehr Büros führen? Vielleicht. Deutschland ist insgesamt jedoch sehr polyzentrisch – von der Bevölkerung her und nicht nur von der „Wirtschaftsstruktur". Vor-Ort-Präsenz ist daher nur mit mehr Büros möglich. Denn wenn die „dezentrale Wirtschaftsstruktur" sich in einem Konglomerat befände (man denke z. B. an Paris), bräuchte ich auch nicht mehrere Büros, um die vielen Mittelständler vor Ort zu bedienen."

Die Teilnehmer haben zusätzlich folgende *eher ablehnende Kommentare* abgegeben:

- „Der Mittelstand ist ein sehr unangenehmer Kunde. Mich überzeugt es nicht, dass die Beratungshäuser so sehr auf den Mittelstand setzen, allenfalls den sehr großen Mittelstand, den man auch von den großen Zentren aus betreuen kann. Eher sind die Großkunden regional diversifiziert, und die Berater folgen ihnen."
- „Andererseits gelten große Teile des Mittelstands tendenziell eher als beratungsfeindlich."
- „Es wird […] viele kleine, inhaltlich und geographisch spezialisierte Beratungen geben."

9.19 Bewertung

Die vorliegende These erfährt in diesem Themenblock die größte Zustimmung unter den Teilnehmern: Sie weist den höchsten arithmetischen Mittelwert und die geringste Standardabweichung auf.

In den Kommentaren wird u. a. auf die hohe Zahl der Ballungsräume in Deutschland, auf das so vorhandene Potenzial zur Einsparung von Reisekosten sowie die werbliche Nutzungsmöglichkeit der Standortanzahl und -verteilung verwiesen. Auch dass unterschiedliche Standorte sich als Vorteil beim Recruiting erweisen („Nähe von Wohn- und Arbeitsort") erscheint erwähnenswert.

Abschluss 10

10.1 Zusammenfassung

Der vorliegende Beitrag hat die hohe Beliebtheit der Unternehmensberatung in Deutschland und insbesondere ihre ausgeprägte Fähigkeit zur Polarisierung sowie die Attraktivität des deutschen Marktes im internationalen Vergleich zum Anlass genommen, Grundlagen, Trends und Prognosen zur Managementberatung in Deutschland darzustellen bzw. aufzubereiten.

Nach einem einleitenden Kapitel wurde zunächst die Dienstleitung Beratung definiert und der Markt durch z. B. seine Volumenentwicklung dargestellt sowie die idealtypischen Beratungsfelder und -formen vorgestellt. Anschließend ist in Kap. 3 das Studiendesign expliziert und offengelegt worden.

In den folgenden Kap. 4–9 wurde für die Thesen jeweils ein Hintergrund skizziert, anschließend die entsprechende These formuliert und die Zustimmung oder Ablehnung der Studienteilnehme zunächst summarisch und anschließend in Form ihrer Kommentare abgebildet. Es zeigt sich, dass bei einigen Thesen ein sehr homogenes Stimmungsbild vorherrscht, bei anderen hingegen eine deutliche Lagerbildung zu beobachten ist: Berater stimmen zu und Kunden lehnen ab oder vice versa.

Dieses abschließende Kapitel fasst den Beitrag nochmal zusammen, zieht ein kurzes Fazit und gibt einen Ausblick auf weitere Fragestellungen.

T. Deelmann, *Managementberatung in Deutschland,* essentials,
DOI 10.1007/978-3-658-08892-7_10

	These:	1	2	3	4	5	6	7	8	9	10	11
Gruppe	*N*											
Berater	*5*	3,40	1,80	3,80	2,60	3,00	2,80	2,40	3,40	2,00	1,60	4,40
Kunden	*4*	1,75	2,75	4,00	3,25	2,75	2,75	3,25	4,00	3,00	3,25	3,75
Marktbeobachter	*5*	2,60	3,80	4,20	3,20	2,00	2,40	3,40	3,20	2,80	1,60	3,80
Gesamt	***14***	**2,64**	**2,79**	**4,00**	**3,00**	**2,57**	**2,64**	**3,00**	**3,50**	**2,57**	**2,07**	**4,00**

Abb. 10.1 Übersicht der Teilnehmergruppen- und Gesamtergebnisse je These

10.2 Fazit

Die Prognosen und Trends zur „Managementberatung in Deutschland" wurden in Thesenform 14 Fachexperten aus Beratungen, Kundenunternehmen und aus Beobachterpositionen im Rahmen einer aus zwei Runden bestehenden Delphi-Studie zur Verfügung gestellt und von ihnen bewertet und kommentiert.

Abbildung 10.1 zeigt die Einschätzungen zu den einzelnen Thesen nochmal in der Übersicht für alle Studienteilnehmer sowie für die drei Teilnehmergruppen Berater, Kunden und Marktbeobachter (mit 5 = „Stimme voll zu" und 1 = „Stimme überhaupt nicht zu").

Die Diskussion um die Thesen wurde ausweislich der oftmals ambivalenten Kommentarstrukturen lebhaft geführt. Während die vorgestellte Marktbetrachtung zeigte, dass der Unternehmensberatungsmarkt in Deutschland nachhaltig wächst und bisher Managementberatung als Feld und Expertenberatung als Form dominieren, hat die Diskussion einige Herausforderungen aufgezeigt und Erkenntnisse herausgearbeitet, z. B.:

- Eine Konvergenz von Beratungsgeschäftsfeldern wird in den Grundzügen wahrgenommen, aber ein totaler Vollzug nicht als wahrscheinlich gesehen.
- Die Automatisierung von Beratungsleistungen wird von Marktbeobachtern stärker erwartet, als von den Beratern selber.
- Die gefühlte Reife der Beratungsbranche wird als hoch wahrgenommen und weicht von der tatsächlichen, ausgedrückt durch den Konzentrationsgrad, sichtbar ab.
- Die Überlegung, dass ein Rollentausch stattgefunden hat, bei dem Berater heute vermehrt die Aufgaben übernehmen, die gestern noch die Kunden erledigt haben und Kunden heute die Kompetenzen anwenden, für die gestern noch Berater beauftragt wurden, findet Zustimmung.
- Die dezentrale Wirtschaftsstruktur in Deutschland wird für die überdurchschnittlich hohe Dichte von Büros der großen internationalen Management- und Strategieberatungen verantwortlich gemacht.

Die Managementberatung muss zukünftig auf aktuelle technische, wirtschaftliche und internationale Trends sowie neue Entwicklungen in der Zusammenarbeit mit ihren Kunden reagieren; sie scheint aber voraussichtlich weiterhin gut positioniert zu sein.

10.3 Ausblick

Für die vorgelegte Delphi-Studie ist zu berücksichtigen, dass es sich bei den Ergebnissen zunächst um eine Momentaufnahme handelt und die einzelnen Werte der Zustimmung oder Ablehnung für ausgewählte Thesen lediglich „für sich" stehen können. Nicht minder interessant als diese Betrachtung aus dem Juli und August 2014 wird auch eine Analyse der Veränderungen im Zeitverlauf sein.

Was Sie aus diesem Essential mitnehmen können

- Der Unternehmensberatungsmarkt in Deutschland wächst nachhaltig; Managementberatung als Feld und Expertenberatung als Form dominieren.
- Managementberatung muss auf aktuelle technische und wirtschaftliche Trends reagieren; sie wird sich aber voraussichtlich weiterhin gut positionieren.
- Das Zusammenarbeitsmodell mit den Kunden wird sich für die Beratung sichtbar weiterentwickeln.
- Als Praktiker, d h. Unternehmensberater oder Kunde, haben Sie einen soliden Blick auf die aktuelle Branchensituation und ihre zukünftige Entwicklung werfen können.
- Als Wissenschaftler, d. h. Beratungsforscher bzw. Dozenten und Studierende, haben Sie aktuelle empirische Ergebnisse erhalten, die in Forschung, Lehre und Lernkanon einfließen können.

T. Deelmann, *Managementberatung in Deutschland,* essentials,
DOI 10.1007/978-3-658-08892-7

Literatur

Zitierte Literatur

BDU (Bundesverband Deutscher Unternehmensberater BDU e. V.) (2014) Facts & Figures zum Beratermarkt 2014/2015. Bonn

Deelmann T, Huchler A, Jansen SA, Petmecky A (2006) Internal Corporate Consulting – Thesen, empirische Analysen und theoriegeleitete Prognosen zum Markt für Interne Beratungen. zu|schnitt005, Diskussionspapiere der Zeppelin University, Nr. 5, Friedrichshafen

Walger G (1995) Idealtypen der Unternehmensberatung. In: Walger G (Hrsg.) Formen der Unternehmensberatung – Systemische Unternehmensberatung, Organisationsentwicklung, Expertenberatung und gutachterliche Beratungstätigkeit in Theorie und Praxis. Verlag Dr. Otto Schmidt, Köln, S 1–18.

Zum Weiterlesen

Für einen allgemeinen und breiten Überblick zur Unternehmensberatung

Deelmann T, Ockel DM (Hrsg, ab 25. Erg.-Lfg.) (2015) Handbuch der Unternehmensberatung. Erich Schmidt Verlag, Berlin

Für eine Einführung in die Disziplin der Strategischen Unternehmensberatung

Bamberger I, Wrona T (Hrsg) (2012) Strategische Unternehmensberatung: Konzeptionen – Prozesse – Methoden, 6. Aufl. Springer Gabler, Wiesbaden

Für eine Zusammenstellung und Kommentierung verschiedener empirischer Arbeiten

Deelmann T (2012) Consulting in Zahlen. Epubli/Holtzbrinck, Berlin

Für eine explizite Forschungsperspektive auf Unternehmensberatung

Nissen V (Hrsg) (2007) Consulting Research – Unternehmensberatung aus wissenschaftlicher Perspektive. DUV Gabler, Wiesbaden

T. Deelmann, *Managementberatung in Deutschland,* essentials,
DOI 10.1007/978-3-658-08892-7

Printed in the United States
By Bookmasters